Art, Aesthetics and Philosophy
Reflections on Coomaraswamy

Hyderabad Studies in Philosophy, no. 11

Art, Aesthetics and Philosophy

Reflections on Coomaraswamy

Editors

S.G. Kulkarni

Kavita Chauhan

INDIRA GANDHI NATIONAL CENTRE FOR THE ARTS

New Delhi

DK PRINTWORLD

Publishers of Indian Traditions

Cataloging in Publication Data — DK
[Courtesy: D.K. Agencies (P) Ltd. <docinfo@dkagencies.com>]

Philosophy of Ananda Coomaraswamy (Seminar) (2011 : University of Hyderabad)
Art, aesthetics and philosophy : reflections on Coomaraswamy / editors, S.G. Kulkarni, Kavita Chauhan.
p. cm. – (Hyderabad studies in philosophy ; no. 11)
Includes bibliographical references.
ISBN 9788124607640

1. Coomaraswamy, Ananda Kentish, 1877-1947 Congresses. 2. Art, Indic – Philosophy – Congresses. 3. Aesthetics – Congresses. I. Kulkarni, S. G. II. Chauhan, Kavita. III. Title. IV. Series: Hyderabad studies in philosophy ; no. 11.

DDC 709.54 23

ISBN 13: 978-81-246-0764-0
First published in India in 2015

Published by:
Indira Gandhi National Centre for the Arts
Central Vista, Janpath, New Delhi - 110 001
Phone : (011) 2338 8438, 2338 8241
e-mail : kalakosa_ed@yahoo.co.in
Web : www.ignca.nic.in

and
D.K. Printworld (P) Ltd.
Regd. Office : *Vedaśrī*, F-395, Sudarshan Park
(Metro Station: Ramesh Nagar)
New Delhi – 110 015-11
Phones : (011) 2545 3975, 2546 6019; *Fax* : 2546 5926
e-mail : indology@dkprintworld.com
Web : www.dkprintworld.com

Printed by: D.K. Printworld (P) Ltd., New Delhi

Foreword

IGNCA understands the arts as comprising of creative and critical literature, written and oral; the visual arts ranging from architecture, sculpture, painting and graphics to general material culture, photography and film; the performing arts of music, dance and theatre in their broadest connotation; and all else in fairs, festivals and lifestyle that has an artistic dimension.

Through its diverse programmes of research, publication, training, creative activities and performances, IGNCA seeks to place the arts within the context of the natural and human environment. The fundamental approach of IGNCA in all its work is both multidisciplinary and interdisciplinary. This work is carried out through five divisions — Kalā Nidhi (Library & Information Division); Kalākośa (Research and Publication Division); Janapada Sampadā (Division for the Study of Diverse Living Traditions); Kalā Darśana (Division for Exhibition and Presentation); and Sūtradhāra (Division for Administration and Co-ordination). It also has a well-developed Media Unit for audio-visual documentation and film-making as also a Cultural Informatics Lab for the production of interactive multimedia CDs, DVDs and developing a National Digital Data Bank on Culture.

In this organizational milieu, the Kalākośa Division of IGNCA has been bringing out three fundamental series of publications, viz.:

1. Kalātattvakoṣa — series of Indian key concepts;

2. Kalāmūlaśāstra — fundamental texts bearing on the Arts; and
3. Kalāsamālocana — a series of analytical and interpretative writings on the Arts.

Out of these, the first is a multi-volume Thesaurus of Indian thought systems and categories of knowledge. These volumes make explicit the multi-disciplinary character of the cognitive reflection that permeates different disciplines and different levels. The six volumes so far published in this series have been enthusiastically received as essential reference material by scholars. The second series is the publication of fundamental texts based on primary materials. These texts range from the earliest discussions on the nature of musical notes to the texts discussing temple plans, town planning, theatre, music and dance. The twenty-six published texts in this series, including some in multiple volumes, throw significant light on the vigorous theoretical traditions of India.

Finally, the third series, under which the present volume is published, comprises publications on analytical and interpretative writings on different facets of the arts and aesthetics. Around sixty works of eminent scholars have already appeared in this series. Some of the major compositions highlight the unbroken artistic traditions of other parts of Asia as well. Bringing out reprints of the collected works of Ananda K. Coomaraswamy is the most important part of this series. Through his prolific writings, Ananda Coomaraswamy revealed himself as a great art critic, philosopher and historian of our time. His son Rama P. Coomaraswamy gave copyright permission to IGNCA to reprint the works of his father. In fact, way back in 1994, a part of the Ananda Coomaraswamy collection was first acquired by IGNCA through the efforts of Dr. Kapila Vatsyayan, former Member Secretary and Founder Member of the IGNCA Trust. She personally met Rama P.

Coomaraswamy in the US and he very generously donated a part of his father's collection. It includes books, photographs, gramophone records, some unpublished papers and slides.

Out of this collection, IGNCA has till date brought out seventeen publications which include reprints of the revised editions of his works, while some are the volumes of his collected papers and letters. A volume of the bibliography of his works also has been published. Details of the published volumes are given in the Preface by Dr Advaitavadini Kaul, Chief Editor, IGNCA, and Coordinator of the Kalāsamālocana Series.

In 2008, IGNCA acquired yet another collection of Ananda Coomaraswamy from Francis Nicholas Coomaraswamy. This collection comprises photographs, paintings, about 700 folders containing correspondence, notes and monographs compiled by Ananda Coomaraswamy during his lifetime.

The publication of the present volume may be seen as the fructification of the efforts of IGNCA in presenting the manifold aspects of this multifaceted personality. It is a matter of satisfaction for us that the idea of holding a seminar on Coomaraswamy emerged through the publications of IGNCA. We are happy to publish the proceedings of this seminar as *Art, Aesthetics and Philosophy: Reflections on Coomaraswamy* which includes eight research papers contributed by eminent scholars in their respective fields. I am grateful to each one of them. My gratitude to Prof. S.G. Kulkarni of the Department of Philosophy, University of Hyderabad for initiating the proposal for organizing the seminar and for bringing it to fruition. Also, I am thankful to him and his colleague Dr. Kavita Chauhan for editing this volume.

Rama P. Coomaraswamy had written a pen sketch of his father for IGNCA. It was published in *Vihangama* (IGNCA Newsletter) in 2001. We find it appropriate to reproduce it here in this volume.

I am pleased to present this volume to the readers with the hope that it will facilitate and enhance the understanding of the concepts of Indian art and aesthetics.

Dipali Khanna
Member Secretary
IGNCA

Preface

In the year 2010 the University of Hyderabad had planned a national seminar on the "Philosophy of Ananda Coomaraswamy". They approached IGNCA with a proposal for publishing the proceedings of the seminar. The seminar was scheduled to be held in February 2011 and was to be organized by the Department of Philosophy. IGNCA welcomed the proposal. For IGNCA, the publication of this volume would have added a new perspective to the Coomaraswamy Series that forms a major part of a publication programme known as the Kalāsamālocana series. We came to know later through Prof. S.G. Kulkarni of the University of Hyderabad that the very idea of holding the seminar had emerged from the extant publications of IGNCA. In a sense, this is a fulfilment of one of the objectives of IGNCA. It is a matter of satisfaction that the publications of IGNCA have motivated scholars and inspired them to reflect upon and discuss the works of a scholar of substance who gave new perspective to the understanding of Indian art and aesthetics.

The Kalāsamālocana series is one of the elemental publication series of IGNCA. It relates to critical writings on different facets of the arts and aesthetics. While one part of the series concentrates on works of eminent scholars who have dealt with fundamental concepts, identified perennial sources and created bridges of communication by juxtaposing diverse traditions, the other part deals with revisions, and rearranged editions and translations of a select number of eminent authors and their works. The most important part of this programme is bringing out the collected works of Ananda K. Coomaraswamy. IGNCA has till date published seventeen volumes of Ananda Coomaraswamy's writings. These volumes have been reorganized thematically, with the author's authentic revisions, and edited by eminent scholars.

In the Cultural Archives of IGNCA the Ananda Coomaraswamy collection has publications of his own writings which comprise many voluminous books, a very large range of pamphlets, articles, critical reviews, translations and letters published in different countries. A glance at the list of his writings indeed makes one wonder whether one is looking through the catalogue of a library or the works of a single individual. Out of this corpus, the details of the seventeen volumes published by IGNCA till date are summed up below:

Philosophical Writings

1. *Time and Eternity* (1990): Man's awareness of Time has been articulated in ancient and modern civilizations through cosmologies, metaphysics, philosophy, religion, theory and arts. Coomaraswamy propounds that though we live in Time, our deliverance lies in eternity. All religions make this distinction between what is merely "everlasting" (or "perpetual") and what is eternal.
2. *Spiritual Authority and Temporal Power in the Indian Theory of Government* (1993, 2013) edited by Keshavaram N. Ienger & Rama P. Coomaraswamy: The Indian theory of government is expounded in this work on the basis of textual sources. The welfare of the community in each case depends upon a succession of obediences and loyalties; that of the subjects to the dual control of king and priest, and that of all to the principle of an eternal law (*dharma*) as King of Kings.
3. *Hinduism and Buddhism* (1999) edited by Keshavaram N. Ienger & Rama P. Coomaraswamy: The two essays are

authoritative expositions on the teachings of these religions as understood by those who practised them rather than as understood by scholars and comparative religionists who studied and viewed them from without.

4. *Perception of the Vedas* (2000) edited by Vidya Nivas Mishra: Coomaraswamy published *A New Approach to the Vedas,* and thereafter he regularly brought out longer and shorter studies of the Vedas and Upaniṣads. Published in a variety of American, European and Indian journals, these essays have been arranged in this volume in relation to some aspect or the other of Vedic text as one integrated perception.

5. *Elements of Buddhist Iconography* (2008) edited by Krishna Deva: This study deals with the basic symbols of Buddhist art, viz., the Tree of Life, the Earth-Lotus, the Word-Wheel, the Lotus-Throne and the Fiery Pillar, and shows that these symbols can be traced back beyond their first representation in Buddhist iconography through the aniconic period of the Brāhmanical Vedas, even into the R̥gvedic period itself, and that they represent a universal Indian symbolism and set of theological concepts.

Writings on Civilizations

6. *What is Civilization?* (1989): The essays raise fundamental questions, which are both piercing and incisive. In one unbroken sweep, a vast spectrum of Western and Eastern civilizations is covered. Four essays in this volume — "Mind and Myth", "Symbols", "Interpretation of Symbols" and "Symbolism of Archery" — reflect the autumnal ripeness of Coomaraswamy's mind journey as an art historian.

7. *Selected Letters of Ananda Coomaraswamy* (1988) edited by Alvin Moore Jr. & Rama P. Coomaraswamy: The letters

included in this volume, published for the first time, reveal the being of this uncompromising man, who believed in no theories or ideologies, political or philosophical issues. Combining scientific precision with his own sensitivity, Coomaraswamy addresses himself to the disciplines of history, philosophy, religion, arts and crafts. The letters reveal the incredible range of his mind which cuts across civilizations, cultures, languages, arts and crafts, encompassing the whole.

8. *A Bibliography of Ananda Kentish Coomaraswamy* (2002) compiled and edited by James S. Crouch: This comprehensive and accurate bibliography is an invaluable reference work for anyone concerned with the study of comparative religion, mythology, traditional metaphysics, iconography and symbolism.

Writings on Art and Aesthetics

9. *Yakṣas: Essays in the Water Cosmology* (1993) edited by Paul Schroeder: The origin of the *yakṣa*s is examined in the context of Vedic, Brāhmanical and Upaniṣadic literature, along with the non-Aryan and pre-Aryan preoccupation with the concept. Dealing with the interpretation levels of artistic motif, Coomaraswamy delves deeper to unfold the water cosmology.

10. *The Transformation of Nature in Art* (1995) edited with an Introduction by Kapila Vatsyayan: In this volume, Coomaraswamy attempts to explain the theory behind medieval European and Asian art, especially art in India. The first principle of his theories is that art does not exist for its own sake; it exists as a means to some religious conditions or experience. He supplements the Indian theory with that of the Chinese. The comparison with medieval European art is also extremely illuminating. He shows that both differ radically from post-Renaissance European Art.

11. *Essays on Jaina Art* (2003) edited by Richard Cohen: Jaina art and its symbolic inventory held a special place in Coomaraswamy's formulation of the history of Indian painting, indeed Indian civilization itself. He was the first to recognize its chronological place in the succession of style. His writings on Jaina art span the entire period of his active working life as an art historian.

Writings on Music

12. *Vidyāpati Padāvalī* (1994) translated by Ananda K. Coomaraswamy: The poetry of Vidyāpati (original in Maithilī) arrested Coomaraswamy's attention for translation, although translation was otherwise the least of his callings. Perhaps he felt the need to convey through the English language the multi-layered symbolism of these seemingly simple verses revolving round the love of Rādhā and Kṛṣṇa. The story of love told in the poems is an allegorical representation of the yearning of the human soul for the Divine.
13. *Thirty Songs from the Panjab and Kashmir* (1994) edited by Premlata Sharma: Indian music was one of Coomaraswamy's several early callings. He endeavoured to look at this art as a major contribution to the world heritage. In 1911, Coomaraswamy along with his wife Alice stayed in a houseboat in Srinagar in Kashmir. Here, Alice became a *śiṣyā* of Ustad Abdul Rahim of Kapurthala who stayed with them for about ten weeks. She recorded the songs and Coomaraswamy translated them into English and wrote an introduction.

    The thirty songs documented here in staff notations by Ratan Devi (Alice's professional name) are compositions of genres like *dhrupad, khyāl, ṭhumrī* and *dādrā*, as well as folksongs in Punjabi, Dogri, Kashmiri, etc., also Sufi songs in Urdu, Persian and Kashmiri.

14. *Essays on Music* (2010) edited by Premlata Sharma: Coomaraswamy held that music in countless ways had been bound up with the Indian national culture, for it was the most universal expression of emotion. He bemoaned that foreign (English) education had paralysed the living impulses of Indians and driven India to a state of social disintegration. He advocated that the restoration of Indian folk and art music to its proper place in Indian education would result in the understanding of the self-expression of India in her music.

Writings on Architecture

15. *Essays in Early Indian Architecture* (1992) edited by Michael W. Meister: Coomaraswamy's probing analysis of texts and sculpted reliefs, in order to reconstruct the extraordinary wooden architecture of early India, was not only an act of great scholarship, but it also laid a foundation on which later histories of India's exceptional architectural tradition have all been constructed.
16. *Essays in Architectural Theory* (1995) edited by Michael W. Meister: This volume presents the essays that best represent Coomaraswamy's rapidly developing thinking on the hermeneutics of architecture — its "why" not "how". These can best be understood in the order in which they were written. The "Kandarīya Mahādeo" (1947) published in the year of his death, placed the form of the temple at the still centre of Coomaraswamy's thought.

Writings on Science

17. *Writings on Geology and Mineralogy: Scientific Papers and Comments* (2001) edited by A. Ranganathan & Srinivasa Rao: This volume deals with A.K. Coomaraswamy's

> contribution to the geology and mineralogy of Ceylon (Sri Lanka). The material in the volume has been arranged in three sections: the first contains his articles on geology and mineralogy of Ceylon published in scientific journals; the second includes the classic Ceylon Administrative Reports which he wrote in 1903-06; and the final section is mainly concerned with several comments on Coomaraswamy's work which highlight his reputation as a mainstream geologist. His greatest contribution to geology was his discovery of the mineral Thorianite in 1904.

From the list of publications given above, a few have already gone out of print. One of them *Spiritual Authority and Temporal Power* was reprinted in 2013. It was released on the occasion of the closing function of the Silver Jubilee celebrations of IGNCA along with a small monograph — *The True Scholar: Passages from A.K. Coomaraswamy on Art and Scholarship*, selected and introduced by Roger Lipsey. Work on reprinting the other (out of print) volumes is already in the pipeline. Alongside that, bringing out more writings from the collection of Ananda Coomaraswamy is also under consideration. Meanwhile, the publication of the present volume on *Art, Aesthetics and Philosophy: Reflections on Coomaraswamy* is a contribution to the IGNCA series on Coomaraswamy at a different level. The scholarly articles of the volume are expected to provide some clarity in understanding the ideas of a great intellectual who, being an enlightening influence in the West, was also instrumental in awakening us to the beauty of our own tradition in the East.

Advaitavadini Kaul
Chief Editor, IGNCA

Ananda Coomaraswamy
A Pen Sketch

*Rama P. Coomaraswamy**

[Dr. Ananda Kentish Coomaraswamy (1877–1947) was one of the most penetrating scholars to live in the twentieth century. His father, Sir Mutu Coomaraswamy (1833-79), was from a prominent Sri Lankan family, and his four uncles' statues adorn the four corners of the Parliamentary Building in Colombo. His father was the first "oriental" to be knighted and was for a while a member of the British Parliament. His mother was English, a lady in waiting to Queen Victoria and herself entitled. He was born in Sri Lanka, but Sir Mutu died of Bright's (kidney) disease when his son was three years old, and his mother, of necessity, returned to England where he was raised.]

A.K. Coomaraswamy's schooling was at Wycliffe College in Stroud, Glochestershire, where his academic achievements were excellent. While there, he taught himself Icelandic and translated one of the shorter Icelandic sagas. He sent this translation to an Icelandic scholar at Oxford who praised it highly and made only one or two minor corrections. The family has this translation, made at approximately the age of

---

* Dr. Rama P. Coomaraswamy (1929–2006) was son of AKC. A Thorasic and Cardio-Vascular Surgeon, he was also Professor of Ecclesiastical History in the St. Thomas Aquinas Seminary in Connecticut, USA. Always maintained his interest in traditionalist metaphysics and in traditional art. He freely gave copyright permission only to IGNCA to reprint the works of his father.

12, with his notes and the corrections. Many years later a visitor from Iceland came to their home and the visitor could not speak any of the European languages or English. AKC spent several hours conversing with him in Icelandic.

Thus it was that his linguistic ability became manifest very early in life. It should be noted that Greek, Latin and French were part of the normal curriculum in those days. Indeed, without the knowledge of both Greek and Latin one could not go on to college. Ultimately AKC was familiar with some 36 languages and by familiarity he once stated that to know a language meant to be familiar not only with its poetry and music, but to be able to read it without a dictionary! I once found him reading a Chinese text, a language which he had not listed among those he "knew". When I asked him why he had omitted it, he said, he still needed to use a dictionary from time to time.

Wycliffe College is located near a quarry, which is one of the best locations in England for collecting fossils. It was only natural that this would result in an interest in geology. This further developed and led to his receiving his Doctor of Science from London University in the field of Geology and Botany — two lifelong interests which he retained. After graduation, AKC went back to Ceylon for the first time and completed a geological survey of the country, which to this day remains a standard work. He also discovered the new mineral Thorianite and was involved in the discovery of another mineral labelled Serendabite. His wide travels in Ceylon led initially to an awareness of the destructive influence of Western values on the land which in turn required a deeper understanding of both Hindu and Buddhist culture — for it was these that were being destroyed. This also led to his involvement in political activities.

He then spent considerable time in southern India where the same forces were at play. It was here he began to write essays on Hindu culture and music, which eventually led to his landmark text on the *History of Indian and Indonesian Art*. He returned to England and wrote, illustrated and hand published on William Morris's press, *Mediaeval Singhalese Art*. The book in its original edition (for it has been reprinted many times) is truly a work of art in itself. Returning to India, he spent several years in the north where among other things, he collected many wonderful examples of Indian Art. He offered these to the then reigning government if they would build a museum to house the collection, but his offer was rejected and so he brought all these wonderful examples back to England.

He was involved in the Indian Independence movement during this period of his life, and his home was frequently visited by individuals whose interests were still associated with Independence movement. During the First World War, he refused to serve in the British army as long as India was under British rule. As a result, he was exiled from the British Empire and his home — "Norman Chapel" — was confiscated and was made part of the English National Park Service. Arrangements were made by an Act of Congress for him to live in America where he remained till his death in 1947. He was able to bring the art collection to America. Obviously, under the circumstances, AKC could no longer by actively involved in such activities. In the United States, he became the Curator of Indian and Oriental Art at the Boston Museum of Fine Arts and also taught courses at Harvard, as well as lectured in various other universities and establishments. He continued his writing — initially primarily concerned with the arts, but more and more with the meaning and purpose of art, and thus with metaphysics. During the last fifteen to twenty years of his life, it was primarily with the latter that his interests lay. And here of course his linguistic ability served him well, for he was able to read in the original the sacred texts of all the great religions. At the same time, he took time to write several striking essays on the socio-economic problems of the world and the continued destruction of true craftsmanship in the name of progress and the garnering of money, a process which has all but come to completion in our days.

There is a passage in Ecclesiastics, which pertains to him in remarkable degree:

> The wise man will seek out the wisdom of all the ancients and will be occupied in the prophets. He will keep the sayings of renowned men, and will enter withal into the subtitles of parables. He will search out the hidden meaning of proverbs, and will be conversant with the secrets of parables. He shall pass into strange countries; for he shall try good and evil among me.

AKC's knowledge of both the Vedas and the theological writings of the Catholic Church Fathers was phenomenal, not just knowledge, but understanding. This enabled him to translate the Sanskrit texts using proper equivalent theological terms such as the most modern Christian theologians are unfamiliar with. Thus his writings in this area are a boon both to Western scholars and to Indians who are seeking to understand their own roots. AKC had no interest in being original, for he was only interested in seeking out the truth which is to be found in these ancient sources, and which are as true today as ever they were. An interesting story: When I was giving a talk at Hawaii University, a young Ph.D. candidate told me he had wished to do his doctorate on my father, but his advisor rejected his request because he said AKC never said anything new. My father would have been delighted with his comment, for the last thing he wished to do was something new.

In 1947, he retired from the Museum and intended to return to India which now being independent, he was free to do. It was his intention to take *saṁnyāsa*. It was shortly before the planned departure that he suffered a fatal heart attack. And so it was only his ashes, which his wife returned to the Ganges. His legacy to India however remains his greatest gift, a legacy in Art, Culture and above all in Metaphysics. And it is this which the Indira Gandhi National Centre for the Arts has so wonderfully been preserving and making available to those who like him are seeking to understand, whether in India or elsewhere in the world.

Contents

Acknowledgement

THE papers collected here were presented at a national seminar on the *Philosophy of Ananda Coomaraswamy* held in February 2011, and was organized under UGC–ASISHH programme of the Department of Philosophy, University of Hyderabad. We are grateful to the University Grants Commission (UGC) for the financial assistance. Our special thanks to the contributors of the papers for their enthusiasm and commitment. We are also indebted to the Administration of the University of Hyderabad for all the facilities extended in organizing the seminar. The editors gratefully acknowledge the support and encouragement received from colleagues, student friends and the office staff of our Department.

We have no words to thank our friends and well wishers at Indira Gandhi National Centre for the Arts (IGNCA), New Delhi, who warmly responded to our request to consider the proceedings of the seminar for publishing. In particular, we cherish the zeal shown by Dr Advaitavadini Kaul, Chief Editor (IGNCA) and co-ordinator of the Kalāsamālocana series. We are highly grateful to Ms. Dipali Khanna, Member Secretary of IGNCA for her support and for writing a foreword to this volume.

Contributors

Prof. Sharad Deshpande,
Tagore Fellow
Indian Institute of Advanced Study
Shimla – 171005
sharad.unipune@gmail.com

Prof. Parul Dave Mukherji
School of Arts and Aesthetics
Jawaharlal Nehru University
New Delhi – 110067
parul.dm@hotmail.com

Prof. Sachidananda Mohanty
Department of English,
School of Humanities,
University of Hyderabad
Hyderabad – 500046
sachimohanty@yahoo.co.in

Prof. Mohan G. Ramanan
Department of English
School of Humanities
University of Hyderabad
Hyderabad – 500046
Mohanramanan1949@gmail.com

Prof. Ranjan K. Ghosh
Formerly Department of Philosophy
University of Delhi
Delhi – 110007
ranjanghosh14@gmail.com

Prof. Archana Degaonkar
Pratap Centre of Philosophy
North Maharashtra University
Amalner – 425401
Jalgaon (Maharashtra)
pratap.philosophy@gmail.com

Prof. R.C. Pradhan
Department of Philosophy
School of Humanities
University of Hyderabad
Hyderabad – 500046
pradhanrameshchandra@yahoo.com

Sarada Natarajan
Researcher in Art History
Hyderabad
sarada.natarajan@gmail.com

Introduction

ONE of the significant developments in the post-independent philosophical scene of India is the recognition that the claim that modern Indian philosophy is either not modern or not Indian or not philosophy was a travesty of truth. Our deep engagement with the nineteenth–twentieth-century Indian savants has convinced us that in spite of their organic link with the classical Indian thought, they were sensitive to the intellectual traditions of modernity, responses to which shaped their concerns and positions on some crucial issues, both time-honoured and contextual. Also, though their orientation was intended to be universal their focus was India and, in particular, the colonial condition against which she had begun to struggle in a way that was unique. Further, their thinking was philosophical in the fundamental sense of a culture's self-understanding, on the one hand, and grappling with the civilizational issues raised by the challenges of modernity, on the other, which sought to determine the values guiding our individual life and the organizing principles of our collective life. In view of such a task, "philosophical" in the discursive sense was irrelevant. It is, therefore, natural that the crux of modern Indian philosophy, unlike that of its Western counterpart, was one of weaving visions rather than building theories. This is evident in the works of Vivekananda, Tagore, Aurobindo, Gandhi and Ananda Coomaraswamy, whose thoughts have rendered the very concept of modern Indian philosophy into a distinct theoretical category.

As pointed out above, the primary focus of modern Indian philosophy was India herself, and even here as a civilization, rather than a nation state, potential or actual. The discovery (and invention for the protagonists of imperialism) of India as a civilization was motivated by (1) an endeavour to seek terms of self-understanding and thereby reject India's characterization by the West including the myth of pre-colonial barbarism; and (2) to convince ourselves that the colonial onslaught could not destroy the cultural self of India, though it might have mauled her socio-economic body.

Obviously, such an endeavour begins by directly confronting the issue of tradition vs. modernity, though such an undertaking might end with transcending that dichotomy as one of those dualities the West has used. to delegitimize and thus domesticate its Other. In doing so, the modern Indian philosophers articulated their idea of tradition that speaks volumes about their creative imagination. Geeta Kapur very ably brings this out when she says:

> What in India we call tradition today was put in the fray by 19th-century nationalists. The manifestos of Swadeshi (political and cultural self-reliance) . . . produced in conjunction with the ideal tradition, a kind of aesthetic which is at once didactic and contemplative. This is best exemplified by A.K. Coomaraswamy. — 1990: 48

Since tradition so construed is another name for Indianness, it was the fulcrum of self-understanding and hence of resistance. The attempt to dive deep into the collective memory of the people and to affirm the value of the extant modes of life was an effort to win back a civilizational poise set at naught by the forces of colonialism. To quote Geeta Kapur again:

> If the savants of the [20th century], among them Coomaraswamy, have excavated the past to provide the present (in their opinion errant and impoverished) century with perennial life-symbols the exercise has rather special

> significance when this is contextualized within an anti-imperialist struggle. — 1990: 50

The national culture construed on the lines of reconfigured tradition was not anchored in the transcendental notions figuring in the Indian metaphysical tradition, though such notions do figure in the articulation of the idea of national culture. We may say these notions were connected to the concrete lives of the people. The Upaniṣadic message was read by Tagore in the art of the folk such as the songs of baul musicians. Vedantic ideas were connected to ordinary people's religious ethos by Vivekananda, thanks to his association with Sri Ramakrishna. Gandhi related truth with the ethos of the productive life of peasants and artisans:

> With Coomaraswamy tradition, besides its metaphysical status, is the code derived from and applied to actual/ideal iconographic forms. — 1990: 50

Hence, there was no need to bring tradition to life as it was alive and in the case of Coomaraswamy, it found living expression in the canonical aesthetic of craftsmen. It was this recognition of the ways tradition finds living expression that goes against their characterization as conservative. Further, modernist dichotomies, such as tradition and modernity and trichotomies, whether conservative, liberal and radical, may help us to understand an intellectual/cultural phenomenon only up to a point beyond which it is detrimental to its authentic understanding, in particular, grasping how a creative thinker defies formulae by the very dynamism of his thinking. More importantly, conservativism merely rejects modernity, it does not work out its critique which points to an alternative vision, and this is precisely how modern Indian thinkers succeeded. Their critique of modernity was at once profound and concrete. Modernity was fundamentality construed in terms of the industrial civilization and the attack on it was cognitive, ethical and aesthetic. That is, the critique portrayed modernity as false consciousness, immoral and ugly. Particularly important in this connection is the vision of a "post-industrial society" — words coined by Coomaraswamy as acknowledged by Arthur J. Penty who used this expression in connection with the concept of Guild Socialism — a concept which found its first expression in the thoughts of those whom Karl Marx called "Patriarchs of Socialism" (cf. Brantlinger 1986: 485). Coomaraswamy contraposes what he called "inspired tradition" that emanates from highest religious consciousness with modern civilization. A society based on the former is a co-operative workshop whose production is geared towards use and not profit. Industrial society, the icon of modern civilizations, replaces needs that can be fulfilled by wants which keep artificially multiplying by transforming human needs into market demands.

We have touched only a couple of issues which Coomaraswamy addresses with matchless intensity and conviction. There are many other issues especially those pertaining to art and aesthetics on which Coomaraswamy took positions. The papers in this anthology critically engage with his positions on these issues. We summarize these papers, as far as possible, in the words of the authors themselves.

Sharad Deshpande in his "Ananda Coomaraswamy and Spiritualization of Indian Arts" begins by asking what happens when two civilizations meet one another under colonial conditions and what makes one civilization interpret the other the way it does? He argues that these questions presuppose a much wider civilizational context of the reception of ideas, values and beliefs on both sides of reception. What makes Ananda Coomaraswamy one of the most central figures in the modern Indian art history is, for Deshpande, his awareness of this larger civilizational context. Therefore, to situate Coomaraswamy in the context of the historical unfolding of the civilizational encounter between India and Europe would be a pre-condition of any meaningful reading of Coomaraswamy. After spelling out some of the details of this encounter Deshpande traces how the construction of an idealistic, spiritualist world-view of Indian civilization and its aesthetic traditions emerged in the writings of E.B. Havell, and following him Ananda Coomaraswamy. According to Deshpande we need to have a theoretical framework to see the interrelatedness of various concepts and doctrines through which the spiritual or the idealistic character of Indian art was inscribed by the colonial scholars of Indian art history.

Parul Dave Mukherji in her paper "The Two Faces of Ananda Coomaraswamy: Discourses on Modernism and Anti-Modernism" focuses on the significance of a reassessment of Coomaraswamy's legacy in our increasingly globalized world. Looking back at the twentieth-century cultural politics, Coomaraswamy emerges as a heroic figure who singlehandedly brought about a profound transformation in taste, sensibility and categories of seeing art. At a time when Asian art was still a beleaguered entity and Indian art did not even feature as culturally significant, Coomaraswamy became a Messiah of the East, a saviour of Indian and Asian art and a champion of an alternative, non-Eurocentric aesthetic. From a post-colonial perspective, it is easy to reclaim Coomaraswamy as an agent of decolonization whose interpretation of Indian philosophy and aesthetics enabled a positive recognition of cultural difference and a radical critique of modernization. However, recently, there has begun a reassessment of Coomaraswamy's legacy in the West that focuses on him as an ardent exponent of modernism. From his role as a defender of Eastern art, today Coomaraswamy's work assumes significance in the history of modernism itself. His close association with the Stieglitz circle, the Euro-American avant-garde and his early acceptance of photography as worthy of a museum collection align him squarely with the modernists. How do these two conflicting constructs of the Coomaraswamian legacy relate to our contemporaneity that is no less ridden with contradictions between universalism and cultural difference?

Ananda Coomaraswamy is studied by Mohan Ramanan in his paper "Aestheticizing the Nation: An Essay on Ananda Coomaraswamy" as part of the national discourse to which Tagore, Gandhi and Radhakrishnan contributed. Coomaraswamy, like others, saw India in ideal and spiritual terms and provided an aesthetic underpinning to this conception of the Indian nation. He reacted to the Western prejudices about Indian art and spoke eloquently about that art as ideal and essential and as representing the soul of India in all its beauty. Coomaraswamy spoke of the origins of Indian art and of its emphasis on the principles of synthesis and unity. The Naṭarāja figure, the dance of Śiva, was for him a classic expression of that principle. That was the artistic expression of India herself. In synthesizing art, philosophy and the nation Coomaraswamy made a signal contribution to India's freedom from the colonial yoke albeit in aesthetic terms.

Sachidananda Mohanty, in his paper, "Polemics of Decolonization: The Art Criticism of Sri Aurobindo and Ananda Coomaraswamy" attempts to show that while the post-colonial critics such as Edward Said, Homi Bhabha, Gayatri Spivak, Aizaz Ahmed and others have unveiled the colonial cartography in ample measure, there seems to be a surprising omission of the earlier narratives of decolonization during the early part of the twentieth century. Many of these seem to belong to the dominant religious/spiritual traditions of the day. Later and more recent approaches have preferred the secular and cultural materialist position. Modern systems of thought have not paid adequate attention to the question of faith and the notion of the sacred. The upsurge in religious fundamentalism worldwide could be one of the many factors that may have caused an intellectual wariness when handling this question. Mohanty argues that there is a need to come up with an alternative theory of decolonization, especially in the realm of art criticism. For, the omission has impoverished post-colonial theory significantly. It has ignored a vital world-view and a significant part of the cultural history of South Asia. Mohanty has closely studied the art criticism of Ananda Coomaraswamy and Sri Aurobindo against the backdrop of decolonization that was central to both the figures.

Ranjan K. Ghosh in his paper "Towards an Understanding of the Aesthetical Philosophy of Coomaraswamy" seeks to bring out the salient points in the aesthetical philosophy of Ananda Coomaraswamy who did pioneering work in this direction and was instrumental in bringing out the significance of Indian art and its grounding on the philosophico-spiritual traditions of our country. For Coomaraswamy artistic creativity is an intensely inward journey undertaken for the purpose of reaching out to the Ultimate Reality. Crucial to this enterprise is the attempt to discover and suggest the idea behind the sensuous appearance. Realism when understood in terms of the imitation of the perceptual world is quite antipathetic to imagination, and it does not find a place in the ideal of Indian art. An important distinction is drawn between ideal beauty and empirical beauty. In Indian art, the ideal of beauty is a beauty of type — one that is formalized and rhythmic. Coomaraswamy raises the question with regard to the ideal of beauty in Indian art and then goes on to clarify the point. An object of beauty is also a source of bliss (*ānanda*). One turns to art for bliss that is lasting and pure or unmixed with pain or suffering. Art, in this sense, is identified as a vehicle of perfect and unmixed bliss. Beauty in nature is partial and not pure, beauty in art is perfect and pure. In this sense, beauty in art is ideal — that which is reconstituted by the imagination of the artist or poet.

Archana Degaonkar in her paper "Ananda K. Coomaraswamy on Art, Culture and Indianness" deals with the four Indian thinkers of the colonial period, namely, K.C. Bhattacharya, M. Hiriyanna, Rabindranath Tagore and Ananda Coomaraswamy who have offered a cogent defence of what might be termed "Indian Aesthetics". Ananda Coomaraswamy offers art criticism using the canons of spirituality. His approach involves a combination of the concepts of traditional art theory as well as the practice of art in India. It also consists of numerous examples to substantiate his point. He emphasized Indian practices related to the viewing of art and invoked the concept of Indian culture as an important factor involved in art appreciation. He anticipated E.H. Gombrich who regarded the "Innocent Eye" of the appreciator as a myth. Coomaraswamy's concept of culture is linked with the significance of workmanship, artisans and craft. An avid admirer of traditional Indian craftsmanship, Coomaraswamy's views on technology are comparable to that of Martin Heidegger. Art for him is bound up with culture and reflects the basic human condition. Traditional Indian art is non-repeatable, exclusive and is something we should actively cherish as our cultural heritage.

R.C. Pradhana in his paper "Coomaraswamy as a Metaphysician" argues that Ananda Coomaraswamy's metaphysics is founded on the Advaita Vedānta to which he was committed in his theory of man and the universe. According to him, the ultimate reality can be described as *sat–cit–ānanda* and that man and universe are the different manifestations of the supreme consciousness, i.e. *Brahman*. Coomaraswamy goes further in showing that the Western religions and classical metaphysical systems hold a similar view of life in depicting the salvation of man as consisting of the realization of the oneness of life and the world. It is this oneness of reality which marks the monistic metaphysics of Coomaraswamy.

Sarada Natarajan, in her paper "The Visual and the Material in Coomaraswamy's Art History" starts by showing that a persuasive idealist approach to art history emerged in India in the early decades of the twentieth century, an anti-imperialist challenge to colonialist discourses in the fields of archaeology, the arts and culture in general. Ananda Coomaraswamy was the most significant theorist of this newly-formulated frame for "Indian Art", a frame encompassing diverse artefactual productions with a wide geographical and historical sweep. Coomaraswamy's writings emphasized the symbolic meanings and metaphysical significance of Indian artistic production, arguing for the unity of Indian art at the level of a shared set of ideals. However, as this paper attempts to demonstrate, this emphasis was achieved at the expense of attention to the irreducible phenomenal specificity of individual artworks, in particular, to their distinctive visual and material qualities. The analysis that follows examines the levels at which these extra-representational, often powerfully "affective", qualities are systematically left out of Coomaraswamy's discourse about pre-modern Indian art. The paper concludes with a few arguments favouring a renewed philosophical engagement with the visuality and materiality of works of art, an engagement that need not be limited by traditional conceptions of aesthetics, whether Indian or Western.

Editors

References

Brantlinger, Patrick, 1986, "A Postindustrial Prelude to Postcolonialism: John Ruskin, William Morris and Gandhism", *Critical Inquiry*, no. **22**.

Kapur, Geeta, 1990, "Contemporary Cultural Practice: Some Polemical Categories", *Social Scientist*, 18(3).

1

Ananda Coomaraswamy and the Spiritualist Reading of Indian Art*

Sharad Deshpande

WHAT happens when two civilizations meet one another under colonial conditions? What makes one civilization interpret the other the way it does? These are the most basic questions which in turn presuppose a much wider civilizational context of the reception of ideas, values and beliefs of both sides of that reception. What makes Ananda Coomaraswamy the "name and symbol to cherish" (Ray 1984: 7) is perhaps his awareness of this larger civilizational context. Therefore, to situate him in the context of the historical unfolding of the civilizational encounter between India and Europe would be a pre-condition of any meaningful reading of Coomaraswamy.

Given this wider civilizational context of the reception of the East by the West and vice versa under the colonial period we need to remind ourselves that most of the prevalent scholarship of Indian art stands largely on the shoulders of the early archaeological and Indological studies in the colonial era, which focused primarily on Indian temple and monumental architecture as well as iconography. While making sense of the Oriental antiquity in general and Indian antiquity in particular, the European scholars faced two

* I am indebted to Dr. Kapila Vatsyayan for insightful discussion on the centrality of Coomaraswamy to modern Indian aesthetic theory. I am thankful to Prof. Shirshendu Chakravarti for critical reading of the first draft.

fundamental problems. First, to devise a theoretical framework and a method in order to determine how one style — for example, the Gupta — was related to another — for example, the Mauryan — in time, unless it was assumed that they coexisted; and second, to make aesthetic evaluations of those styles. At a philosophical level the resolution of these issues required that history be linear so that various "stages of development" and "styles" of architectural monuments, e.g. caves and temples, can be differentiated from one another. At a concrete level of investigation it required a new kind of methodology in contrast to the traditional indigenous methods of Indian art history. The new framework and the method were "modern" because they were based on different conceptions of knowledge, presuppositions and beliefs, history, and in particular, conceptions of aesthetic norms of beauty that were different from those of Indian origin. It gave a different perspective from which to look at, to understand, and to interpret Indian art, particularly Indian temple architecture as well as other sites found in excavation at different places. Based on its own presuppositions, and in contrast to the Oriental conceptions of art and beauty, the European interpretative exercise in its initial phase portrayed Oriental monumental architecture as "monstrous".[1] But the colonial understanding

[1] The dichotomous European interpretations of Indian art, viz. the "monstrous" vs. "spiritualist" dominate the colonial experience of viewing and appreciating Indian architecture. The origins of viewing the Oriental archaeological sites as monstrous is located in the early fourteenth century when the European travellers, unable to comprehend the massive rock-cut Buddha figures at Bamiyan in Afghanistan, viewed the Buddha figures as "monstrous". James Fergusson consciously adopted this characterization of Indian arts in his archaeological studies. On the other hand, the spiritualist interpretation of Indian architecture can be located in Ram Raz *Essay on the Architecture of Hindus* (1834) which was further developed into a rigorous metaphysical doctrine by E.B. Havell and Ananda Coomaraswamy.

of Indian art, in its later phase, interpreted not only Indian temple architecture but also all Indian art as "idealist", "spiritualist" or "divine". However, for the European mind, being "monstrous" or "spiritual" meant primarily something that could not fit into European consciousness. The history of the Indian arts based on such ascriptions is in fact a condensation of the ideas of Romantic Nationalism, the theories of the German and the English Orientalists,[2] the empirical accounts of historical sites given by the British administrators in India, the archaeological survey conducted by European scholars and the historical accounts given by them. The "history" of Indian aesthetic tradition that emerges from the works of European scholars is thus a result of how the West, through its own categories of understanding, its own biases and prejudices, its own historically determined privileged position, and with its economic and political interests, has perceived and interpreted India's culture and civilization. Before one interprets Indian art in terms of the European world-views such as "classical", "medieval", "idealistic", "realistic", "naturalistic", "transcendental", "divine spirit", etc. it must be remembered that these ascriptions not only characterize Indian art but make a *statement* on the nature of Indian culture as a whole.

But though culture is something that is identifiable, something about which we can talk concretely, it is, in an important sense, not a regimentation of peoples' beliefs and practices. While interpreting Indian aesthetic traditions as spiritual, we need to remember that India has neither a single homogeneous tradition nor a homogeneous social set-up. Since there have been a large number of diverse traditions and cultures that have interacted with one another and flourished together in this subcontinent, it is but natural that the resulting

---

[2] George Birdwood, John Ruskin and William Morris idealized the village crafts in India as if they were in antithesis to history in general and the Industrial Revolution in particular.

"forms of life" were quite complex and interactive. The co-existence and interaction between various world-views that are based on different, and sometimes even opposite metaphysical presuppositions — held by the Advaitins, the Buddhists, the Jainas, the Cārvākas, the Naiyāyikas and the Sāṁkhyas — do not warrant any blanket statement about Indian culture in any one singular ascriptive mode such as "spiritual" or "material". It is interesting to note that until recently the historiography of Indian philosophy was based on an oversimplified binary between *āstika* (orthodox) and *nāstika* (heterodox), blurring the immense variety among the *āstika*s and *nāstika*s.

What the Europeans meant by "spiritual", "ideal" or "divine" is not just a lexicographer's concern. The exact equivalent terms in Sanskrit or any other Indian language must be ascertained. What is required is a much more rigorous and perceptive reading to find out how Western scholars looked at Indian civilization and its culture. This "new" understanding offers a certain kind of interpretation of Indian aesthetic traditions and is evident in the works of James Mill, William Jones, Vincent Smith, General Cunningham, Alfred Foucher, Mount Stuart Elphinstone, James Fergusson, Ernest Binfield Havell, Sister Nivedita and Kakuzo Okakura. We need to place Ananda Coomaraswamy in this broad framework within which even the post-Coomaraswamy art historians like Stella Kramrisch, Radhakamal Mukherjee, Niharranjan Ray, Vasudev Sharan Agarwal, S.N. Dasgupta, Kapila Vatsyayan and many others have worked. They have constructed an idealistic, spiritualist world-view of Indian civilization and its aesthetic traditions, in their own ways. In order to comprehend the emergence of this world-view we need to have a theoretical framework to see the interrelatedness of various concepts and doctrines with which the spiritual or the idealistic character of Indian art was inscribed by the colonial scholars of Indian art history. For this purpose we may invoke Edward Said's doctrine of Orientalism.[3] It is a generic term used to describe (a) a systematic discipline of learning, discovery and practice, (b) coming to terms with the Orient in terms of the European colonial experience, and (c) a Western way of restructuring and dominance over the Orient. Within this framework we can further distinguish between the early and the later, the authoritarian and liberal varieties of Orientalist approaches to Indian art. Thus, we can distinguish between the authoritarian biases of the early Orientalists like James Mill, Thomas Macaulay and James Fergusson from those of the later liberal-minded Orientalists like William Jones, E.B. Havell and Coomaraswamy. Within this framework, on the one hand, we can make sense of the putative idealistic or spiritualistic interpretation of Indian art, and on the other, the creation of such institutions as the Asiatic Society,[4] the Archaeological Survey of India,[5] the Madras School of Art and Bombay Art School[6] which became the foundations for the teaching, research and archiving of Indian art. To understand the present-day history of Indian art, it is important to understand the prejudices of the early Orientalists

---

[3] Said is relevant only to the extent to which he highlighted the prejudices of the European scholars towards Indian art.

[4] The Asiatic Society of Bengal was established in 1784 with Sir William Jones as its first Director. This was followed by the establishment of the Asiatic Society of Bombay in 1804 with Sir Mackintosh as its Director.

[5] The Archaeological Survey of India was established in 1870 with Sir Alexander Cunningham as its first Director.

[6] The Madras School of Art was established in 1850 and The Bombay Art School was established in 1857 with the initiative of Sir Jamshedjee Jeejeebhoy.

like James Fergusson,[7] Alexander Cunningham;[8] the French Scholar Gabriel Jouveau Dubreuial[9] and the counter-perspectives of liberal Orientalists like Havell and Coomaraswamy.

The early and the later Orientalists differ on two important issues: (a) foreign influence on Indian art, and (b) classification of Indian arts. The issue of foreign influence further raises three questions: (1) were there shared codes in which Indian culture exchanged the aesthetic ideas with those of other cultures — from the Greco-Roman to the Egyptian, Persian and Chinese cultures? (2) did aesthetic ideas emerge only from Greece and Rome and did the Indian artists and artisans move by copying them? and (3) were Indian aesthetic ideas and ideals purely indigenous, neither interacting with other cultures in terms of shared codes, nor being dominated by the Greco-Roman style?[10] The second issue concerning classification of

---

[7] James Fergusson (1808-86): a figure of greatest importance in introducing the scientific study of Indian architecture. He recognizes that "there is not only one Hindu or one Mohammedan style in India, but several species of each class, that these occupy well-defined local provinces, and belong each to certain ethnological divisions of people". But his studies are charged with Anglo-Saxon racial prejudices and have a denominational basis for classifying Indian architecture as Buddhist, Jaina, Hindu and Mohammedan.

[8] Alexander Cunningham (1814-93): the founder of the Archaeological Survey of India. Influenced by Darwinian Evolution Theory, he classifies Indian art as Indo-Grecian, Indo-Scythian and Indo-Sassanian.

[9] Gabriel Jouveau Dubreuil (1885–1945): Introduced the method of comparative study of Ornaments.

[10] The most prominent point of reference in this problematic view was the contrast in styles between the Buddha images made at Gandhara and Mathura. This debate continued from the old Orientalists to Havell and Coomaraswamy. While the old Orientalists claimed superiority in the Greco-Roman style of the Gandhara image, liberal Orientalism claimed the superiority of a contemplative true Indian style of the Mathura Buddha image. Likewise, the Maurya Lion →

Indian arts pertains to the methodology of classification. How is it possible to classify Indian arts according to dynasties, or religions, or aesthetic styles, or economic development of societies? These two issues of foreign influence and foreign classification of Indian art forms determined the early attempt to understand the history of Indian aesthetic traditions.

Whereas the early Orientalists viewed Indian art and aesthetic traditions from the orthodox Oriental point of view, not excluding the racial superiority complex, Ernest Binfield Havell[11] is considered important as he inaugurated liberal Orientalism in Indian art history. Coomaraswamy in 1910 called him "the beginning of a new order of things" (1910: 289-90). Havell is unique in so far as he is a major and significant departure from the earlier archaeological approaches towards Indian art heritage, as evident in the works of Fergusson, Cunningham and others. His four magnum opuses[12] are indicative of his liberal interpretation of Indian culture. His main focus was on reviving India's art heritage. But more importantly, because of his seemingly holistic appreciation of

→ capital at Sāñcī was claimed to be Grecian art by Cunnigham when he said that king Aśoka employed Greek artists. The theory of the Greek influence on India is evident also in James Princeps' "Discovery of the name of Antiochus the Great in two edicts of Asoka, King of India" and in Alfred Foucher's *L'Art Greco-Bouddhique du Gandhara*. John Marshal, Director General of the Archaeological Survey of India, in early twentieth century, said that the Mauryan lions show Hellenic influence which was clearly "speculative" and stated that aesthetic inspiration came from a mixed Iranian and Hellenic spirit in Bactria.

11 Ernest Binfield Havell (1861–1934) was superintendent of the School of Industrial Arts at Madras (1886-90) and Government School of Arts at Calcutta (1897–1906). He was the most prominent champion of a deeper understanding of Indian fine arts and Indian style of painting.

12 *Indian Sculpture and Painting* (1908), *The Ideals of Indian Art* (1911), *Indian Architecture: Its Psychology, Structure and History from the First Mohammedan Invasion to the Present Day* (1913) and *The Ancient and Medieval Architecture of India* (1914).

Indian art and aesthetics which is covered under the generic term "spiritual", Havell emerges as a prelude to Coomaraswamy and therefore it is essential to get at Havell's approach to Indian art and especially the idealistic–spiritualistic turn that he gave to Indian art history. This turn is so decisive that it portrays almost every art form, be it architecture, dance, music, sculpture, painting or any other every art activity as exemplifying the Divine Spirit. Havell's attribution of idealism and mysticism to Indian art lies in (a) the attitude of European scholars towards the Orient, and (b) the specific mode of the application of historical, political and epistemological paradigms of the Western traditions to the study of India. The three forces — historical, political and epistemological — outlined as the Orientalist point of view, determine this horizon of translation which affixes the predicates of idealism, spiritualism and mysticism onto Indian culture. Responding to the early Orientalists like James Mill's ridiculous claims that art needs intellect and crafts require skill, and that Indian fine arts were unnatural and offensive or George Birdwood's disturbing remarks in 1910 on a Javanese Buddha figure displayed in the gallery of the Royal Society of Arts[13] with their racist sub-text, or Cecil Burns' announcement that Indian art is dead, Havell chose to study Indian art in a passionately Indian manner. While the distinction between "arts" and "crafts" took a prominent form especially in the Bombay School Report (1869-70), the passion in Havell drove him to critique the fundamentals of the British viewing of Indian arts. The cluster of distinctions such as "art" vs. "craft", "fine" vs. "applied", "sculpture and painting" vs. "decorative arts",

---

[13] "The senseless similitude, by its immemorial fixed pose, is nothing more than an uninspired brazen image, vacuously squinting down its nose to its thumbs, knees and toes. A boiled suet pudding would serve equally well as a symbol of passionate purity and serenity of soul."

"high arts" vs. "articles of domestic use", "decorative" vs. "ornamental", was prominent in the early Orientalist critique of Indian art which denigrated Indian art as being merely decorative or ornamental and not having the status of "high art" as judged by the European standards. Historically, the above distinctions can be located only in the period of industrialism from the mid-1750s. These distinctions were drawn in Europe and were made only in the eighteenth century, before which the distinction between artists and craftsmen was not valid. It is also doubtful whether such distinctions ever existed in the history of Indian aesthetic theories prior to the eighteenth century. Havell, and later on Coomaraswamy, stressed that these distinctions were drawn by those prejudiced against Indian arts. Havell disagreed with Birdwood's one-sided appreciation of the merely decorative element in Indian art, which denied the status of genuine art to Indian sculpture and painting. He argued that Indian aesthetics treats decoration as an integral aspect of sacred architecture. Indian "spiritualism" was able to unite what the British classicists like Birdwood divided: fine arts from ornamental arts. The battle lines were drawn between the classicists who drew hierarchical divisions in and amongst various arts and the romantics. Like William Morris before him, Havell chose the latter method which sought a unifying picture of all art forms. Like Morris he refused to accept the division in arts, such as the "great arts", i.e. sculpture and painting, and the "lesser arts", i.e. decorative arts.

The challenges posed to the Western hegemonic interpretation and understanding of Indian art are to be placed in the wider context of multifarious changes that were taking place all over the world. It is not a sheer historical accident that these challenges were concurrent with the chain of events taking place outside colonial India, e.g., the Slavophils' revolt against Western individualism in Czarist Russia, and

Vivekananda's discourse in America — the citadel of pragmatism and hedonism — where he proclaimed a radical spirituality. Unlike the revolutionary Marxists who were struggling against the capitalist and imperialist hegemony in the political sphere, "spirituality" seemingly became the answer to British colonialism in India. Havell, Coomaraswamy and Margaret E. Noble, the Irish woman turned Sister Nivedita (a disciple of Swami Vivekananda) formed a triumvirate that sought an Indian "spiritual identity". The discovery of this Indian identity reversed the ideologies of the "monstrosity" of the early Orientalists into that of a spiritual identity. The "meaning" of Indian civilization was conceived by way of presenting ancient Indian art as spiritual. Spirituality became the dominant ideological mode of interpretation where Havell was able to intervene in the colonial discourse initiated by the early Orientalists who were stressing the binary opposition between the "Orient" and the "Occident". Though Havell did not radically depart from this root binary opposition, his and such other interventions were inspired by the twentieth-century reversal of European authoritarian ideology. Between 1901 and 1902 Okakura,[14] the disciple of Ernest Fenellosa,[15] wrote the pan-Asian document, *The Ideals of the East* (1904).[16] In the preface to this book Sister Nivedita claimed that "Asia is one". Asia became the common denominator *vis-à-vis* hypostatized constructed Europe. These were the attempts to have a holistic picture of civilizations. Like Hegel they claimed that the truth lies in the whole. But unlike Hegel they conceived

---

14 Kakuzo Okakura (1862–1913), a renowned Japanese critique of Westernization.

15 Francisco Ernest Fenellosa (1853–1908), American Art Historian of Japanese Art.

16 Herein Okakura argues that broad expanse of love for the Ultimate and Universal, which is the common thought inheritance of Asiatic races, enabled them to produce all the great religions of the world.

their discourse in its binary form. The "whole" that Orientalism seeks to comprehend is thus a "whole" without parts — i.e. a construction of a pan-Asia devoid of historical details of specific nations. This "whole" is then viewed as transcending binaries by erasing one pole within each binary set. Thus the "subject" erases the "object". The idea of the whole is thus the idea of a formalized and idealized reality. Havell, Sister Nivedita, Okakura and Coomaraswamy in their respective ways apply this technique of abstract holism to political and aesthetic theories. These interventions are further characterized by positing transcendence not only into the specific work of art but onto the artistic expression or onto art as such. For example, while interpreting the icons of the Buddha and Śiva images, Havell observes that they have a "divine essence" which is composed of the "spirit". In this form of characterization, the work of art stands negated from the concrete human and historical conditions. It posits the "symbolic" and the "transcendental" levels of meaning as constitutive conditions for the work of art if it is to be significant at all. Havell's main focus is thus to inscribe ideal divinity onto the Indian arts. The Indian artist is portrayed as seeking the "divine essence" or "spirit", striving to realize something of the universal, the eternal and the infinite.

While the British Orientalists from Fergusson to Birdwood could appreciate only certain facets of Indian arts, Havell's holistic understanding of Indian aesthetic tradition is expressed under the generic term "spiritual". Havell is thus a prelude to the most of the contemporary understanding of Indian art. But it is Coomaraswamy who provides the master text. While both Havell and Coomaraswamy understood India as spiritual, Coomaraswamy's method is radically different from that of Havell. In his review of Havell's *The Ancient and Medieval Architecture of India*, which appeared in the *London Times*, Coomaraswamy describes Havell's method as "bewildering, because so many difficult and complex problems are solved with such apparent ease, and yet the working out of the problem is rarely supplied" (cf. 1915a).

Although Havell offers a spiritualist understanding of the Indian arts, spiritualism as such is not a homogeneous category and the concept of spiritualism is itself expressed in various ways. Spiritualism primarily refers to a certain outlook and is generally contrasted with materialism, which again is not a homogeneous category. Both these terms mean different things in different contexts. Again, it is not clear whether there is any term in classical Sanskrit that comes close to the concept of spirit or spiritualism as it is used in the Western tradition. In the colonial context, anything that did not conform to the Western parameters of rationality was generally contemptuously dismissed as "non-rational" — a blanket term for superstition, faith, occult and spiritual. Despite these difficulties Coomaraswamy develops a complex reading of Indian art in terms of spirituality which has influenced generations of Indian artists and art historians. This complexity is understood in terms of a combination of rigorous sociology, transcendental metaphysics and a profound understanding of Indian art history. The Coomaraswamy scholars and Indian art historians often stress the underlying contradictions in his being a social philosopher who was defending a strong nationalism while being the historian and interpreter of Indian art and culture. However, as Niharranjan Ray claims:

> . . . The fact remains that until very recent years most writers on Indian arts and aesthetics, both Indian and Western, including myself, have more or less followed the tracks laid down by him. It is Coomaraswamy who is mainly responsible for the fact that Indian activities in creative art have very largely been frankly literary and ideological. It was he who seemed to have furnished the theory and intellectual inspiration on which came to be based the revival

> of our art activities during the first three decades of this century. Even today Coomaraswamy remains a source to which one inevitably turns for an understanding of Indian arts and aesthetics. — 1984: 7

Coomaraswamy is called a man of two cultures; Occidental and Oriental, guild socialist and medievalist, sociologist and metaphysician. Despite these apparently dualistic strands, Coomaraswamy formed a "Perennial Philosophy of Mankind" (Lipsey 1977: 274-78). As he claimed, "I want to serve not merely India but humanity and to be as absolutely universal as possible-like the *Avalokiteśvara.*" (Mitter 1994: 260) A man of great learning, Coomaraswamy knew archaeology, ethnology, history, natural sciences and metaphysics. His knowledge of languages spanned Sanskrit, Pāli and Prākṛt to Greek, Latin, German, French and English. Disenchanted with modern industrial civilization, his deep commitment to tradition and his deep distrust of everything that is modern formed the basis of his philosophical methodology as well as empirical method of investigation. His disenchantment coincided with that of a great number of European intellectuals and artists like Richard Wagner, Thomas Mann and the early Georg Lukas who expressed their discontent with modern civilization. The romantic disenchantment with modern civilization is rooted in:

1. Tonnies' distinction between *Gemeinschaft* (community) and *Gesellschaft* (society), the former being understood as a living organism while the latter as an artificial and commodified society based on economic and legal contract (cf. Tonnies 1955),
2. the nineteenth-century Romantic distinction between *Zivilization* and *Kultur* (ibid.), and
3. the consequent romantic nostalgia for medieval society. In 1913 Coomaraswamy was exposed to the dominant intellectual ideas — Nietzsche's philosophical impact in

England, the revival of William Blake and the underlying theme of anti-industrialism. Anti-industrialism made Coomaraswamy:

> . . . a devout medievalist committed to a medieval structure and organization of society in which manual labour and manual arts and crafts play the most dominant role from the point of view of productive economy. — Ray 1984: 7

Unlike Rabindranath Tagore who could synthesize traditional values with the demands of modern society, Coomaraswamy refrained from any such synthesis.

The two basic elements in Coomaraswamy's researches are (a) the scientific, i.e. descriptive and empirical method, and (b) the ideological interpretation of traditional culture and society. The former has shaped his engagement with actual works of art, the corresponding time periods and societal structures; for instance, the destruction of Kandyan art in colonized Ceylon. The latter led him to form the idealized view of history. Coomaraswamy's idealization of history, i.e. of medieval society, and of Indian art comprises three elements:

1. philosophical idealism which is transcendental in character and metaphysical in aim and purpose. In this brand of idealism the transcendental character that is attributed to art erases the human and social content of art;
2. ideological *Weltanschauung* which develops philosophical idealism in terms of and in relation to the idealization of medieval society. In this world-view medieval society is presented as a perfect, just and ideal society. As the Sri Lankan art historian Senake Bandaranayke observes, these "metaphysical ideas — divorced from their real social context — forms the basis of his (Coomaraswamy's) later philosophical writings" (1984: 33). This idealization of medieval society also posits a

disputed view of the anonymity of the artist in medieval India, while holding the view of an Utopian guild system. Indian aesthetics, what Coomaraswamy called "uncaused spiritual activity", is to be viewed as a process without an empirical or historical subject; and

3. idealization of history which understands *Itihāsa* as myth (1943: 3). Myth according to Coomaraswamy is not a social discourse or a poetic invention but "the penultimate truth" of which all temporal events are said to be mere appearances. Myth is thus claimed to be universal but at the same time capable of expressing itself in diverse points of views.

These three idealizing strands become prominent in the following passage from Coomaraswamy's reiteration where he extols an idealized past:

> Ideal futures . . . (could be) built . . . (where there are) only heroic subjects, subjects that are impersonal, devoid of topical interests, and at the same time universal in their context, (which are) the warp and the woof of the web of the cosmic consciousness, (and) the true basis of a national or universal art. — 1909: 301

And again, on aesthetic idealization of the visual image in Indian art wherein Coomaraswamy argued for a symbolic and mathematically ideal icon:

> The Indian or far-eastern icon, carved or painted, is neither a memory image nor idealization; but a visual symbolism *ideal in the mathematical sense.* The anthropomorphic icon is of the same kind as a *yantra*, i.e., the geometrical representation of a deity or *mantra*, i.e., an auditory representation of a deity. Accordingly, the Indian icon fills the whole field of vision at once; all is equally clear and equally essential; the eye is not led to range from one point to another, as in empirical vision, nor seek a concentration

> of meaning in one part more than in another as in mere "theatrical art". There is no feeling of texture or flesh, but only of stone, metal or pigment, the object being in one or the other of this material and not a receptive replica of any objective cause of sensation. — Subramanian 1984: 17

Coomaraswamy's idealistic aesthetics and ideological affiliations to medievalism form the epistemological basis of his works. His critique of British imperialism's destruction of Sri Lankan arts which he witnessed in 1903 after his return from England led him, unlike the French Utopians, not to a revolutionary critique of commodity production and the possibilities of a futuristic vision of society, but to a hypothetical past which convinced him that feudalism is a just and democratic society. In his *Medieval Sinhalese Art* Coomaraswamy recalls Okakura's idea of "spiritual feudalism where caste makes a peasant in all his poverty, one of the aristocrats of humanity" (1956: 31). Explication of the ideological superstructure of Coomaraswamy's spiritual medievalism reveals the rich texture and composition of his works. From Ruskin he learnt that "industry without art is brutality" (1981a: 29), and with the coming up of industrialism and capitalism, "Iron had entered the soul of man" (Jagmohan 1984: 167). Coomaraswamy protests against this condition of the mechanization and dehumanization of humanity. This dehumanization underlined the shift from the inner spiritual essence of man to his conditioned outer ego. It is the understanding of this fragmented and divided self on which modernity is based that forms the infrastructure of Coomaraswamy's works. In this tapestry, Coomaraswamy stresses the specificity of the Oriental world-view. Unlike the European view of man and nature Coomaraswamy conceptualized an Indian anthropo-centric attitude:

> The Indian anthropocentric attitude is not really like that of the European. For the European consciousness has never

> been able to realize intuitively the unity of all life, and is hampered by the old Semitic animism that discovers in man a soul that does not exist in animals and trees. . . . European art divides the consciousness of man from that of nature. The Indian artistic tradition is that of a race that finds the individual self in every living thing and even in what some would call inanimate, and so it easily recognizes and sometimes exaggerates the essential likeness of animals and men. — 1976: 71

Division and dissonance of Occidental modernity are here contrasted with a unified conception of life which Coomaraswamy claimed to have existed in pre-Renaissance Europe and in traditional India. The history of India is contrasted with European modernity and its passion for an empiricist division of subject and object, humanity and the world. Thus:

> . . . from the Indian (metaphysical) and scholastic points of view subjective and objective are not irreconcilable categories, one of which may be regarded as real to the exclusion of the other. Reality (*satya*) subsists there where the intelligible and the sensible meet in the common unity of being, and cannot be thought of as existing in itself . . . but rather as knowledge or vision . . . — 1981b: 7

In this unified life–world, Coomaraswamy portrays Orientalism as religious, symbolic and literary. He inquires into the metaphysical questions of Indian art. He claims that there is a common metaphysical basis of all religions. He studies the genesis, classifications and internal developments of each art form. Coomaraswamy's major achievement in the history of Indian aesthetic traditions is the discovery of the principle of the "internal development of each art form" (1926: 165). From this vantage position he could subvert the doctrine of foreign influence on Indian art which was hegemonized by the old Orientalists like Foucher and Fergusson, who claimed that Greek and Roman influences had inspired the formation of the plastic arts in India. Consequently, the question of the origin of the Buddha image that was stated to emerge from the Appolian idea was not treated, as in Havell's work by suggesting that the Mathura model was more authentic than the Gāndhāra one. Coomaraswamy never claimed that the figures of Buddha were first made in Mathura and later copied in Gandhara. On the contrary, "every element essential to the iconography of Buddha and *bodhisattva* figures appears in early Indian art before the Buddha figure of Gandhara or Mathura is known" (Bhattacharya 1984: 63).

On the chronological character of the Buddha images Coomaraswamy distinguishes early Buddhist art which is "truly Buddhist" from "an art about Buddhism" which cease to be truly Buddhist in spirit and character" (ibid.). The art *about* Buddhism emerged only when the figure of the Buddha was introduced in art. This is what Coomaraswamy calls "the art about Buddhism". Coomaraswamy distinguishes the authentic Buddhist art from the art about Buddhism in terms of the non-representational and idealistic character of the former. This meant that the Buddha figure could not be represented in any human form due to early Buddhist conception of the *bodhisattva*'s primary resolve to conquer death on the night of the Awakening. Being immortal the *bodhisattva* could not be represented in human form. The spiritual non-bodily type of art thus entered Coomaraswamy's thinking. This spiritual disembodied aesthetics is stated by Coomaraswamy quoting Śukrācārya's *Śukranītisāra*:

> To make human figures is wrong, or even unholy. Even a mis-shapen image of God is always better than an image of man, however beautiful. — 1981a: 31

Coomaraswamy then continues:

> The doctrine here so sternly stated means, in other words,

> that imitation and portraiture are lesser aims than the representation of ideal and symbolic forms: the aim of the highest art must always be the imitation of the intimation of the Divinity behind all forms. One may, for instance, depict the sport of Krishna with the *gopis*, but it must be in the spirit of religious idealism, not for the mere sake of sensuous imagery. — 1977: 84-85

The ideal type in Indian art forms is consequently constructed through the Oriental way of seeing. This vision is understood in Coomaraswamy's reading of the *Dhammika Sutta* as:

> Form, sound, taste, smell, touch, these intoxicate beings; cut off the yearning which is inherent in them. — 1981a: 30

Coomaraswamy stresses imagination and memory and not imitation of appearances. He then conceives of a subjective idealist philosophy of nature that comprehends spiritual inwardness in which Indian art forms are said not to represent nature:

> It cannot be too clearly understood that the mere representation of nature is never the aim of Indian art. Probably no Indian sculpture has been wrought direct from a living model, or any religious painting copied from life. Possibly no Hindu artist of the old schools ever drew from nature at all. His store of memory pictures, his power of visualization and his imagination were for his purpose finer means; for he desired to suggest the Idea behind sensuous appearance, not to give the detail of the seeming reality that was in truth but *māyā* (illusion). For, in spite of the pantheistic accommodation of infinite truth to the capacity of the finite minds, whereby God is conceived as entering into all things, Nature remains to the Hindu a Veil, not a revelation; and art is something more than mere imitation of this *māyā*, it is to manifest what lies beyond.
>
> — ibid.: 21-22

Thus, unlike its modern Western counterpart, Indian art is not an imitation of an object actually seen at a particular point of time, but is in fact, a work of the visionary imagination. The "visionary imagination" thus becomes the essence and leitmotif of Indian art.[17] The question is not that of art being "true to nature". "Truth" and "reality" are not conceived in the form of a sensuous reality or an "external form of nature" (ibid.). Natural forms are only "incarnation of ideas, and each is but a complete expression" (ibid.). Thus, for Coomaraswamy:

> It is for the artist to portray the ideal world of true reality, the world of imagination, and not the phenomenal world perceived by the senses. — ibid.: 24

Coomaraswamy thus enjoins the Orientalist method of visualization that is firmly in opposition to the Western academic style of (i) naturalism, (ii) illusionism, and (iii) the Greek philosophy of mimesis. For "imitation and portraiture are lesser aims than the representation of ideal and symbolic forms: the aim of the highest art must always be the intimation of the Divinity behind all forms, rather than imitation of the forms itself" (ibid.: 31). Like Havell he argues that the physical and the phenomenal "real" have to be erased to posit the "imaginary" and the "symbolic":

> Symbolism must be briefly spoken of. Most familiar, but often more exclusively of religious than of artistic significance, is the use of concrete attributes and symbols, such as the serpent garland, the *triśūla*, and the tiger verses. More subtle is the symbolism of posture of body or position of the hands: the body in activity or in repose, the hands beseeching, granting, destroying, or in some posture of uttermost abstraction. All this symbolism composes an

---

17 However let us not forget that when Aristotle talks about mimesis he means idealization of actuality. So idealization may not be an exclusive characteristic of Indian art.

> expressive art speech so easily understood by those familiar with it.
> — ibid.: 30

Coomaraswamy's symbolism operates on a distinct two-tier structure which is implicit in his works: (i) the social base in which he outlines the genealogy of craftsmen as found in his *The Indian Craftsman* (1909), and (ii) the metaphysics of art which arises from the social foundation of his Utopian genealogy. The social Utopianism that has idealized the pre-industrial society conceives of a unity of humanity and the world. In this ideal type there are no distinctions between fine arts and applied arts, between religion and the secular world, or between the mental and the physical world. The more Coomaraswamy idealized medievalism the greater the proportion of the metaphysics of art forms found in his works. The theme of the unity of life and art derived from socialist philosophies has great methodological importance for Coomaraswamy. According to him when this unity is disturbed there is crisis in art. This crisis reflects (i) decadent art forms, (ii) fragmentation of the arts, and (iii) empiricist and nominalist categories in aesthetics like the category of taste. In *The Transformation of Nature in Art* (1981b) he asserts that taste emerges only with the alienation of art from life:

> To speak of art — exclusively in terms of sensation — is doing violence to the inner man, the knowing subject; to extract from Eckhart's thought a theory of taste (*ruci*) would be doing violence to its unity.
> — ibid.: 49

It seems that Coomaraswamy operates not with the concept of *unity* of subject and object, art and life, but with the idea of *identity* of subject and object. Coomaraswamy bases his theory of the ideal determination of the arts on the identity of subject and object and the primacy of consciousness. What is meant by the "ideal determination of the arts" is the transcendent character of the arts, in which the inner mental vision is represented and where "the self perceives the Self". In order to transcend the fragmented world, Coomaraswamy takes recourse to contemplation that unifies the subject with the object and this type of contemplation Coomaraswamy identifies with *yoga* in which the artist externalizes his inner vision:

> The maker of an icon, having by various means proper to the practice of Yoga eliminated the distracting influences of fugitive emotions . . . proceeds to visualize the form of the *devatā* . . . aspect of God. — 1981b: 3

This method is carried out from "a great distance". It is a "true-knowledge–purity aspect" that "reveals itself against the ideal space" (ibid.). Coomaraswamy thus firmly believed in the spiritual unity of India, holding the view that different religions were mere "dialects of a common spiritual language". This belief became the basis of the idea of a common source of different cultures. This shared basis rendered irrelevant the questions of borrowing and thereby negating the old Orientalist ideologies of the Mathura Buddha as borrowed from the Grecian ideal. Coomaraswamy's paradigm would assert that they are not "borrowed"; they emerge from this shared Oriental ideal.

This extremely deep and critical insight led Coomaraswamy to assert that shared codes presented not merely an Oriental ideal but a basis for World History:

> The Indo-Sumerian and Indo-Iranian background . . . prepares us for the recognition of many common elements in Early Indian and Western Asiatic arts. And in fact a great variety of motifs found in Maurya, Śuṅga, and early Āndhra arts, and thus anti-dating the age of Hellenistic influence, present a Western Asiatic appearance, suggesting parallels in Sumerian, Hittite, Assyrian, Mykenean, Cretau, Trojan, Lycian, Phoenician, Achaemenid and Scythian cultures. A partial list of such motifs would include such mythical monsters as wind lions, centaurs, griffous, tritous: . . . Altar,

> or battlement, friezes, of Bharbut and Orissa . . . lotus or "bell" (so called "Persepolitan") capital. . . . These and others, such as the fret, spiral, volute, labyrinth, and swastika have survived in folk art upto modern times and are widely distributed in India and Ceylon. — 1927: 11-12

Coomaraswamy further gives the examples of the cylindrical *stūpa* with drum in two stages, as seen at Bedsa and in the Kuṣāṇa period which is identical in form with the Phoenician Tomb in North Syria (ibid.: 12). Coomaraswamy further elaborates that there is little in Indian decorative art that is peculiar to India, and India shares a great deal with Western Asia (ibid.: 13). For:

> India, in centuries and perhaps millenniums BCE, was an integral part of an "Ancient East" that extended to the Mediterranean to the Ganges Valley. In this ancient world there prevailed a common type of culture, which may well have had a continuous history extending upwards the stone-age. . . . The effect of these considerations is to withdraw India from its isolation, as a background to the existing art there is a: "common early Asiatic art, which has left its uttermost ripple marks alike on the shores of Hellas, the extreme west of Ireland, Etruria, Phoenicia, Egypt, India, and China." All that belongs to this phase of art is the common inheritance of Europe and Asia. Its various forms as they occur in India or elsewhere at various periods up to the present day are to be regarded as cognates rather than as borrowing. — ibid.: 13-14

Despite this critical understanding of world history Coomaraswamy's commitment to the mystical highlights a certain tension in his approach to Indian art.

By 1910 idealization of Indian arts reached its zenith in terms of principles and method. While Havell and Coomaraswamy as the chief architects were responsible for this idealization process, their differences were also obvious in explaining the social base of Indian aesthetics, in understanding modernity and the philosophical aesthetics of the future. Whereas Havell desired an unchanging Indian tradition Coomaraswamy viewed Indian tradition not in fixed and static terms, but in a volatile state. Roger Lipsey's distinction between the Eastern Coomaraswamy and Western Coomaraswamy becomes relevant here (1977: 107). His theoretical encounter with the ideas of Blake and Nietzsche during 1912-16 provided the philosophical rigour for the critique of modernity and the volatile condition of tradition. He almost echoed Fichte's diagnosis of modernity as "the age of absolute sinfulness", an age in which mechanized environments destroyed the creative spirit of humanity.

Coomaraswamy finds the solution to the dehumanization of the human spirit in *Post-Industrialism,* the term that he invented. In 1914 he co-edited with A.J. Penty, *Essays in Post-Industrialism: A Symposium of Prophecy Concerning the Future of Society*. The specificity of history, the nature of change and Coomaraswamy's anarchist ideas were spelt out in this work.

Coomaraswamy argued for the break-up of industrialism. In this respect he shared ideals with the British Utopian Robert Owen. His disagreement with Marxism was fundamental. According to Marx, society had to absorb the fruits of industrialization for use and consumption. What needed to be changed was the social structure or the mechanism of production, while enriching the productive forces. On the other hand, for Coomaraswamy what needed to be critiqued was the character of the forces of production itself, while retaining the feudal structure of society. In feudalism, Coomaraswamy notes:

> . . . the different parts of the social organism were fitted and dovetailed together; there was a place for every man, and no man could be spared; class distinctions were not invidious, nor emphasized by differences of culture. — 1956: 28-29

From the feudal structure of society, Coomaraswamy inscribes the theory of the artist as a radical *swadeshi* praxiologist: It is the work of poets (poet, painter, sculptor, musician, "artist"– all these are synonyms) to make their hearers free: it is they alone who establish the status of nations (1911: 111-12).

For poets are "our guides to take us back to the elemental and real things of life" (ibid.: 114). In the *Religious Foundation of Life and Art* (1914), the artist is sketched as a Nietzscheian superman, a being that is no longer an anti-religious nihilist. On the contrary, Nietzsche's dictum, "God is dead" is reversed. Idealistic individualism and aristocratic–aesthetic individualism become the essential terms for Coomaraswamy:

> Artists are the priests of every new church; for it is essentially their consciousness that perceives intuitively the unity of all life, which forms the sole test and sanction of all new moralities. . . . Man must obey the deep and often scarcely expressed will, . . . (i.e. the obedience to superman, to a soul-over-individual-man (for how can Superman be a man?) . . .
>
> — ibid.: 104

Post-industrial praxis thus differentiated Havell's and Coomaraswamy's methods. For Coomaraswamy the medieval Utopian Guild ideal was the basis of his aesthetics, whereas for Havell it was the common race ideal, in the Aryan idealized identity between Britain and India. As he says in his *Aryan Rule*, the fate of the British Empire is bound up with the Eastern (or Indian) question. Havell's common Aryanized ideal type necessitated a British–India unifying link. British politics had to be more liberal. For Coomaraswamy, on the other hand, the British had to go:

> There can be no true realization of political unity until Indian life is again inspired by the unity of national culture. More necessary, therefore than all the labours of politicians, is National Education. We should not rest satisfied until the

> entire control of Indian education is in Indian hands. It is a matter in which no European should have a voice, save by the express invitation of Indians. Only those who sympathize can educate. Every government and missionary college and school must be replaced by colleges and schools of our own, where young men and women are taught to be true Indians. — 1981a: iii-iv

The mission of the emancipation of India lay with the artists, for

> . . . nations are made by artists and by poets, not by traders and politicians. Art contains in itself the deepest principles of life, the truest guide to the greatest area, the Art of living.
>
> — ibid.: ii

The year 1909 in which the *Essays in National Idealism* appeared, was the year of radical praxis. The Blakean years 1912-16 in England was the time when the idea of the religion of the future was formed. The years 1932-47 in America were the years of scholarly solitude. These three periods form three definite stages of his intellectual evolution, from the young Coomaraswamy who practised *swadeshi* idealism, to the English years of idealistic individualism, and the Boston years as curator and Scholar. *Time and Eternity, Introduction to the Art of Eastern Asia, A New Approach to the Vedas: An Essay in Translation and Exegesis, Asiatic Art* and *The Christian and Oriental or True, Philosophy of Art* were written in the Boston period. In *A New Approach to the Vedas* Coomaraswamy outlines the principles of *philosophia perennis:*

> What I call here "a new approach to the Vedas" is an exposition of Vedic ideas by means of a translation and commentary in which the resources of other forms of the universal tradition are taken for granted. . . . I have simply used the resources of Vedic and Christian scriptures side by side. An extended use of Sumerian, Taoist, Sufi and Gnostic sources would have been at once possible and

> illuminating, but would have stretched the discussion beyond reasonable limits. As for the Vedic and Christian sources, each illuminates the other. . . . Whatever may be asserted or denied with respect to the "value" of the Vedas, this at least is certain, that their fundamental doctrines are by no means singular. — 1933: vii-ix

From radicality to medievalism, from aesthetic politics to the metaphysical scholarship of what he called the museum militant, Coomaraswamy's intellectual journey has been a long one. His ideas can be summarized from his 1915 essay *Love and Art*:

> Life under modern Western culture is not worth living, except for those who are strong enough and well equipped enough to maintain perpetual guerilla warfare against all the purposes and idols of that civilization with a view to its utter transformation. — 1915b: 574

Coomaraswamy's reconstruction of the Indian aesthetic tradition and his work in making it a vital part of his engagement with his immediate context needs much more attention. To quote Bandaranayke:

> It is precisely this . . . gap between ideas and realities — that has resulted in a separation into two distinct and isolated streams, of the way in which Coomaraswamy's work is received today: the one concerned only with his philosophical ideas and the other, with his art-historical writings. Ironically, the former is more or less restricted in its impact to a small audience, in those very industrial societies which he stood out against, while the latter, stripped of its social dimensions, has formed the basis of a great deal of art-historical studies in South Asia over the last 75 years. — Bandaranayke 1984: 35

References

Bandaranayke, Senake, 1984, "Anand Coomaraswamy and Approaches to the Study of Traditional Sri Lankan Art and Society", in *Parokṣa: Coomaraswamy Centenary Seminar Papers*, ed. Gulam Mohammed Sheikh et al., New Delhi: Lalit Kala Akademi.

Benjamin, Walter, 1982, 'Edward Fuchs': Counter and Historian in the Essential Frankfurt School Reader, New York, ed. Andrew and Gebhardt.

Bhattacharya, D.C., 1984, "Coomaraswamy on Buddhist Art and Iconography" in *Parokṣa: Coomaraswamy Centenary Seminar Papers*, ed. Gulam Mohammed Sheikh et al., New Delhi: Lalit Kala Akademi.

Coomaraswamy, A.K., 1909, *Monthly Review* **6**(3).

———, 1909, *The Indian Craftsman*, London.

———, 1910, "Discussion (on E.B. Havell seminal paper titled Art Administration in India)", *Journal of the Royal Society of Arts*.

———, 1911, *Art and Swadeshi*, Madras: Ganesh and Co.

———, 1915a, "Review of Havell's, *The Ancient and Medieval Architecture of India*", *The Times*, 2 March, London.

———, 1915b, "Love and Art", *Modern Review* **14**(11).

———, 1926, "The Indian Origin of Buddha Image", *Journal of the American Oriental Society*, **46**(2): 165.

———, 1927, *History of Indian and Indonesian Art*, New York: Dover.

———, 1933, *A New Approach to the Vedas*, London: Luzac.

———, 1943, *Hinduism and Buddhism*, New York: Philosophical Library.

———, 1948, *The Dance of Shiva: Fourteen Indian Essays*, with Introductory Preface by Romain Rolland, Bombay: Asia Publishing House.

———, 1956, *Medieval Sinhalese Art*, 2nd edn., New York: Pantheon Books.

———, 1976, *Rajput Painting*, vol. 1, Delhi: Motilal Banarsidass.

———, 1977, *Selected Papers*, vol. 1, ed. Roger Lipsey, New Jersey: Princeton University Press.

———, 1981a, *Essays in National Idealism*, New Delhi: Munshiram Manoharlal.

———, 1981b, *Transformation of Nature in Art*, New Delhi: Indira Gandhi National Centre for the Art.

Jagmohan, 1984, "Contemporary Relevance of Ananda Coomaraswamy", *Parokṣa: Coomaraswamy Centenary Seminar Papers*, ed. Gulam Mohammed Sheikh et al., New Delhi: Lalit Kala Akademi.

Lipsey, Roger, 1977, *Coomaraswamy, His Life and Works*, Princeton: Princeton University Press.

Mitter, Partha, 1994, "Arts and Nationalism", Cambridge: Cambridge University Press.

Okakura, Kakuzo, 1904, "The Ideals of the East: With Special Reference to the Art of Japan", New York: E.P. Dutton & Co.

Ray, Nihar Ranjan, 1984, "'The Life' of Coomaraswamy: An Interpretation", in *Parokṣa: Coomaraswamy Centenary Seminar Papers*, ed. Gulam Mohammed Sheikh et al., New Delhi: Lalit Kala Akademi.

Raz, Ram, 1834, "Essay on the Architecure of Hindus", London: Royal Asiatic Society of Great Bretain and Ireland.

Subramanian, K.G., 1984, "The Significance of Coomaraswamy's Ideas in Our Times", in *Parokṣa: Coomaraswamy Centenary Seminar Papers*, ed. Gulam Mohammed Sheikh et al., New Delhi: Lalit Kala Akademi.

Tonnies, Ferdinand, 1955, *Community and Association*, London: Routledge and Kegan Paul.

2

The Two Faces of Ananda Coomaraswamy
Discourses on Modernism and Anti-Modernism

Parul Dave Mukherji

IN this paper, I will reflect upon two moments of re-reading Coomaraswamy's contribution to the study of Indian culture in which philosophy remains one of the strands. One of the moments coincides with Coomaraswamy's centenary in 1977 when Lalit Kala Akademi organized a conference to mark this passage of time and subsequently brought out a volume of seminar papers titled *Parokṣa*.[1] This publication was preceded by important publication of Coomaraswamy's papers edited by Roger Lipsey in three volumes, one of them being Coomaraswamy's biography.[2] While *Parokṣa* was largely hagiographical, it opened some space for a critical appraisal and assessment of contemporary relevance of his writings in the 1980s. After these two remarkable sets of publications on Coomaraswamy, there seems to have been a lull in interest in his works.

It is again by the closing of the first decade of twenty-first

---

1 Gulam Mohammed Sheikh, K.G. Subramanyan and Kapila Vatsyayan (eds.), *Parokṣa: Coomaraswamy Centenary Seminar Papers*, New Delhi: Lalit Kala Akademi, 1984.

2 Roger Lipsey, *Coomaraswamy: His Life and Work*, vol. III, Bollingen Series, Princeton: Princeton University Press, 1977.

century, that Coomaraswamy begins to loom large in the Western imagination, as attested by two special panels organized at the College Art Association in 2010, the most prestigious forum for Art History in North America.[3] My own investment in Coomaraswamy's writings took the form of the critical historiography when I took up critical edition of "Citrasūtra" of the *Viṣṇudharmottara Purāṇa* in the late 1980s. It was the arduous process of textual criticism that revealed to me the thrust of ideology that underpinned his work and hence I will place my own interpretation of Coomaraswamy's contribution. My take on Coomaraswamy is primarily through the lens of an art historian. Coomaraswamy was involved in art history around the turn of twentieth century during strong colonial presence, philosophy entered his domain as a means to ward off colonial misrepresentations of traditional Indian art. Wholly conversant with the Kantian and the Hegelian legacies of art discourse, Coomaraswamy countered in interesting ways what he saw as the West's misrepresentation of Eastern art. The defect, he alleged, did not lie with the objects of art which were deeply endowed with aesthetic value but with the frameworks for viewing art. Coomaraswamy underlined the West's bigotry in reducing the culturally unfamiliar to familiar terms — in short, their blinkered refusal to engage with the other.[4]

Tribute to Coomaraswamy in the Parokṣa Volume

Paying homage to Coomaraswamy, some of India's leading art historians, art critics and practising artists underlined the

[3] For the first time in the history of the College Art Association conferences, there were two panels organized around "Ananda Coomaraswamy and Influence on Twentieth Century Art" by Lise Kjaer and Will Wroth in Chicago in 2010. I participated on these panels as a discussant.

[4] Parul Dave Mukherji, *The Citrasūtra of the Viṣṇudharmottara Purāṇa*, New Delhi: Indira Gandhi National Centre for the Arts and Motilal Banarsidass, 2001, pp. xxxiv-xlv.

significance of this towering genius who had broken new ground in the study of Indian painting, sculpture and architecture at a time when art history was still a nascent discipline in India. While the main focus was on the contribution by Coomaraswamy to the study of traditional art practice, there was also a section that assessed his role in contemporary times, particularly in relation to modern art. Whereas on the whole, the transcendentalist legacy of Coomaraswamy was celebrated as his unique contribution whereby he gave a new dignity to Indian art, there were only a few critical voices that questioned his conceptual premises.

Out of twenty-seven contributors who expressed their debt to Coomaraswamy in fields that ranged from Buddhist studies, Asian art, Rājpūt painting and Jain painting to Indian aesthetics, the most clearly defined critical stances were taken by artist and ideologue, K.G. Subramanyan and art critic, Geeta Kapur. These two essays strove to read Coomaraswamy's legacy against the grain.

Striking at the heart of Coomaraswamy's position, K.G. Subramanyan highlights Coomaraswamy's famous assertion.

> What representation imitates is the idea or species of the thing, by which it is known intellectually, rather than the substance of the thing as it is perceived by the senses.[5]

To Subramanyan, the problem lay in the way Coomaraswamy "intellectualized the artistic function and held sensation and what he called sentiment in low esteem".

Likewise, his response to Coomaraswamy's conception of the Indian icon is critical:

---

[5] Cited from *The Transformation of Nature in Art* by A.K. Coomaraswamy, New York, 1956 in "The Significance of Coomaraswamy's Ideas in our Times" by K.G. Subramanyan, in *Parokṣa* p. 17.

> . . . Indian icon fills the whole field of vision at once . . . There is no feeling of texture or flesh, but only of stone, metal or pigment, . . .[6]

Subramanyan challenges Coomaraswamy's discomfort with sensuality of Indian art and points out:

> Can we compare an icon of devī or Durgā, resplendent in her physical attributes, to *Śrīyantra*? Can we compare the dynamic statuary of Śiva Naṭarāja to a stone *liṅga*?[7]

Finally, he concludes his assessment of Coomaraswamy thus:

> . . . no historical study especially of a pioneer, cannot be of immutable value, as the passage of time brings new facts and materials in our ken and they amplify our horizons. . . .[8]

Likewise, in her article, "On the Vocation of the Artist", Geeta Kapur reflects on the relevance of Coomaraswamy's writings to modern art. Exploring how he imagines the iconography of traditional artists, Kapur highlights how philosophy — what appears to me as Vedāntic philosophy — guides Coomaraswamy's construct:

> Coomaraswamy quotes the *Śukranītisāra* where it says that the Indian imagist must be an expert first and foremost in contemplative vision (*yoga-dhyāna*), and the act of technique or labour is to set down what has thus been conceived. The conception itself should be of such intensity that the knower and the known come to merge.[9]

Zeroing in on the concept of Self-Noughting upheld by Coomaraswamy, Kapur examines how this underscored the manner in which the traditional artist was valorized over the

---

[6] *Parokṣa* p. 17

[7] Ibid.

[8] Ibid., p. 16.

[9] Geeta Kapur, "On the Vocation of the Artist", in *Parokṣa*, p. 148.

modern artist. For this, Coomaraswamy not only draws support from Indian philosophy but also medieval Western scholastic tradition. Through the concept of *līlā*, Coomaraswamy brings out the disinterested nature of creative act. Just as the divine creativity was out of sheer exuberance and not with any end in view, so is human creativity defined in such a way that desire for worldly merit has no place. And this is how the traditional artist is kept away from the modern artist whose narcissistic obsession with his individuality and personality counters pure disinterested creativity.

In her critique of Coomaraswamy, Kapur projects him as an anti-modernist who was cut off from his own time. According to her:

> Once his concern for social transformation came to be subsumed in a metaphysical scheme, Coomaraswamy naturally felt less and less need for relating to his own age and the actual social issues it generated. What is curious of course is that even had he taken up what we called the lost possibilities — socialism after Morris, or the Gandhian alternative — he would hardly have come closer to the modern. Morris had spoken of his everlasting hatred of modern civilization; Gandhi's hatred was even further charged with the experience of colonial injustice. There was, then, something of a pressing tendency, a predisposition in Coomaraswamy *against* the modern. (Geeta Kapur's emphasis)[10]

Coomaraswamy's Claims of Transcendentalism *vis-à-vis* the Citrasūtra

Around the 1930s, Coomaraswamy felt an urgent need to seek support for his transcendental interpretation of Indian art from traditional textual sources and in this venture, Śilpaśāstras received his keen attention. If his contemporary art historian,

10 *Parokṣa*, pp. 150-51.

Stella Kramrisch's interpretations of Indian art had a dominant formalist thrust, Coomaraswamy looked upon his role as a contextualist art historian who recognized that Western misunderstandings about Indian art lays precisely in the archaeological approach of the colonial art historians which failed to capture the underlying meaning in Indian art.

Indian philosophy offered Coomaraswamy a powerful tool not only to explain the cultural context of art production but also the aesthetic intentionality of the artist. Often, this contextualist approach led him to engage with Śilpaśāstras that were at times too driven by the technicality of art production — sometimes lacking in metaphysical depth. It was from Indian philosophy that he sought to provide depth to otherwise arid technical treatises on art. Some of these texts posed corrupt passages that challenged his efforts at interpretation. My brush with Coomaraswamy's writings happened at a time when I was working on the critical edition of the "Citrasūtra" of the *Viṣṇudharmottara Purāṇa* in 1988. Undergoing training as a textual critic, it often intrigued me as to why Coomaraswamy singled out the shortest of the nine *adhyāya*s of the Citrasūtra — an *adhyāya* most problematic in terms of corrupt passages. It was this chapter that concerned the classification of paintings and the value attached to the role of representation in visual arts in India. Indian art had suffered at the hands of colonial art historians who were reluctant to accord the status of fine art to it on the grounds of lack of naturalism. Prior to Coomaraswamy's confrontation with this text, he had arrived at a conclusion that mimesis was given least priority in Indian art, the aim of which was to offer a transcendental experience.

The Citrasūtra: A Founding Moment in Indian Art History

Coomaraswamy's defence of Indian art preceded his encounter with the Citrasūtra. The very existence of this text, therefore presented a tremendous challenge to his views on Indian art with its use of terms, which could be taken as an open endorsement of "naturalism". Confrontation with this text created a gap between his expectations and the text. It interpellated him in such a way that there remained two alternatives open for him —

1. a radical paradigmatic shift which entailed abandoning the transcendentalist claim for Indian art and recognizing that interest in nature was not rejected by this treatise on art, whichever way nature was understood; and
2. refusal to accept the text at its face value and "discovery" of a deeper and a more significant level of interpretation. Thus the semantic discrepancy had to be negotiated by hermeneutics, i.e. by the act of interpretation, which was a radical strategy for conserving the text that was thought to be too precious to repudiate.

Nevertheless, the text undergoes an alteration without being erased and aberrant meanings are contained within the dominant ideological framework.

Unlike a textual critic, he was not drawn to the textual problems of diagnosing suspect readings and offering emendations. But his project was more grandiose. "What situation could prompt this curious project of transforming a text? The task of interpretation is virtually one of translation in which Coomaraswamy seems to suggest that *X* is really or really means *Y* or that *Y* is really *B*. Interpretation thus presupposes a discrepancy between the clear meaning of the text and the demands of the (later) reader."[11] It seeks to solve that discrepancy. The situation is that for some reason (as hinted above), a text has become unacceptable; yet it cannot be discarded.

[11] Parul Dave Mukherji, 2001, p. xxxvii.

Let us turn to a specific instance of Coomaraswamy's translation of the first type of painting referred to in the text as *satya*:

> *yatkiñcid lokasādṛśyam tat satyam ucyate* |
>
> Painting that represents any of the worlds (*kiñcillokasādṛśyam*), . . . is called Pure or Sacred (*satya*).[12]

It was through a deft management of the text that *satya* comes to be translated as "pure or sacred". The question to be asked at this point is not about measuring the distance between this interpretation and a literal translation of *satya*. Rather, what constitutes the condition under which *satya* has to be translated as "pure or sacred"? *Satya* could no longer be accepted as "true (to life)" as translated by Stella Kramrisch.[13] Prior to his confrontation with the Citrasūtra, Coomaraswamy had been committed to the view that what marks pre-modern Indian art as different from the Western was its intrinsic transcendentalism. On the other hand, the very terminology in the text, if allowed to keep its literal meaning, would strongly contest the metaphysical claim. That is, adherence to a particular construct of naturalism foreclosed acceptance of naturalism as a legitimate category of Indian art.

Another term, which posed this problem, was *sādṛśya*, which had to be negotiated:

> If we understood *sādṛśya* . . . to mean "illusion" or "realism", verisimilitude of any crude or naïve sort, we should be contradicting all that we know of the Oriental conception of art.[14]

It was the coexistence of *satya* with *sādṛśya* (resemblance/

---

[12] A.K. Coomaraswamy, "Viṣṇudharmottara Chapter XLI", *Journal of American Oriental Society*, vol. 52, 1933, p. 13.

[13] Stella Kramrisch, "A Treatise on Indian Painting", *Journal of Department of Letters*, **2**(1924), pp. 1-56.

[14] A.K. Coomaraswamy, 1933, p. 21.

likeness), which compounded the problem of "literal translation". He regrouped the words separating *yatkiñcilloka* and *sādṛśya* against the general rule of Sanskrit syntax to yield the meaning "any of the worlds". This would help him explain away the naturalistic potential in the term *sādṛśya*. If a painting can aim to imitate any of the worlds, traditionally assumed to be three, then imitation cannot have any empirical meaning:

> So also in verse two above, where *kiñcilloka* must include *devaloka* [means abode of gods], *sādṛśya* cannot be interpreted as "naturalistic".[15]

None of the Sanskritists has taken such a liberty with grammar and syntax. V. Raghavan, Coomaraswamy's contemporary, was the first to raise a serious objection to the translation of *satya* as "pure or sacred".

Following this criticism, Coomaraswamy revised his translation of *satya* from "pure" and "sacred" to "intellectual" and "ideal" on grounds of precision. As he says:

> My former renderings "pure" and "sacred" (*JAOS*, 52: 13, etc.) are not incorrect but less precise than "intellectual" or "ideal".[16] — 1933b: 26

Coomaraswamy evidently felt the need for more support for his elimination of the concept of resemblance than the Citrasūtra could provide. He began to look to the idealist schools of Upaniṣadic philosophy to arrive at a metaphysical reworking of the term *satya*.

> *Satya* is "real", "actual", "intelligible", "ideal"; *nāmarūpa*, "form" as distinct from the natural disorder (*anṛta*) of the sensible world (*loka*) (*Bṛhadāraṇyaka Upaniṣad* 1.6.3; *Taittirīya Upaniṣad* II.6).[17]

---

15 Ibid.

16 A.K. Coomaraswamy, "The Painter's Art in Ancient India: Ajanta", *Journal of the Indian Society of Oriental Art*.

17 Ibid.

Certainly, Coomaraswamy's transcendentalist claim of Indian art and aesthetics did not remain uncontested as demonstrated by V. Raghavan's criticism of Coomaraswamy's interpretation and also by other translators of the Citrasūtra.[18] However, such voices of dissent were relegated to the margins and rarely made an impact within the disciplinary framework of Indian art history where Coomaraswamy's theoretical framework retains a canonical status.

Ananda Coomaraswamy's Influence on Twentieth Century

Lise Kjaer and William Wroth organized two panels on *Ananda Coomaraswamy's Influence on Twentieth Century* at the last 2010 College Art Association Conference in Chicago where I was invited to join two panels as a discussant. What needs closer attention is the contemporary interest in Coomaraswamy. Never in the history of the College Art Association Conference has Coomaraswamy aroused such a stupendous interest. While in the former colonies, Coomaraswamy has long been regarded as the great champion of Eastern art and as the one who restored non-Western art to its rightful place in world art, this very contemporary obsession with Coomaraswamy is truly intriguing to me. His entry into the global stage is to be celebrated as attested by the very title of the two panels: *Ananda Coomaraswamy's Legacy and Influence on Twentieth Century Art*.

From his role as a defender of Eastern art, today Coomaraswamy's work assumes significance in the history of modernism itself. Perhaps an efflorescence of our interest in Coomaraswamy springs from our very contemporaneity — the fact that today globalization has brought cultures together as never before and at the same time it has thrust the question

[18] V. Raghavan, "Some Sanskrit Texts on Painting", *Journal of Indian Historical Quarterly*, 9, pp. 898-911.

of cultural difference right into our faces. Such a state of affairs has thrown open a re-engagement with comparativism. No wonder cultural difference has acquired a certain inevitability and salience that makes Coomaraswamy a compelling figure in our own times.

The papers on the first panel explored two distinct facets of Coomaraswamy; while Johannes in bringing out Coomaraswamy's influence on Alice Boner projects the more familiar Coomaraswamy — the one who inaugurated the transcendentalist discourse on Indian art, the majority of the papers highlight not just the formative influence of modernism on Coomaraswamy but how he himself shaped some of the central concerns of modernism.

Johannes focuses on how the lens of transcendentalism through which Coomaraswamy viewed Indian art as largely symbolic and spiritual came to be used by Alice Boner, a Swiss sculptor, art historian and art collector. Alice Boner belongs to the school of Western thinkers who seek in Indian culture an alternative space for art and creativity and inevitably slip into the role of cultural ethnographers. In her quest for true meaning, she uses formalism as a way to pare down the external trappings to arrive at a true meaning located in the core of the image and its symbolic meaning. She transforms Coomaraswamian transcendentalism into metaphysics of form. When it comes to the subjectivity of the Indian artist, Alice Boner appears to conform not so much to Coomaraswamy's model as the one invented by Stella Kramrisch. The notion that the Indian artist is "not the creator, but the transmitter" a mediator rather than inventor echoes in the formulations by Kramrisch where she claims:

> He does not depict the shapes of nature but nature itself, the creative, creating power.[19]

[19] Stella Kramrisch, "The Representation of Nature in Early Buddhist Sculpture", *Rupam* 8, 1921, p. 7.

Johannes also concludes with a lament that Coomaraswamy's influence on our interpretation of Indian art remains almost unquestioned in our times. At this point, I had to point out that critical reassessment of Coomaraswamy's legacy in Indian art history was very much underway and dates back to 1984 when Coomaraswamy's centenary volume titled *Parokṣa* came out. The view that traditional Indian art celebrated the anonymous and selfless *śilpī* (artisan) is increasingly viewed as a myth and new evidence collected by R.N. Mishra about names of the artists compel us to rethink this Coomaswamian commonplace!

Bringing out the astounding modernist face of Coomaraswamy, Catherine Hoffman presents him as a pioneering champion of photography. It was eye-opening to learn from her that it was Coomaraswamy who took the initiative in giving photography a new credibility as worthy of museum collection. The intense conversation between Coomaraswamy and Stieglitz attests to this inaugural moment when photography began to be accorded an avant-garde status. What are even more revealing are the terms of valorization of photography by Coomaraswamy that were steeped in traditionalism which privileged symbolism over verisimilitude. For one familiar with Coomaraswamy's transcendentalist rhetoric and his commitment to spirituality, this recasting of photography in symbolic terms makes one rethink the modernist project. Coomaraswamy's circle of friends in New York consisted of the most progressive modernists of the time who were instrumental in introducing the United States to European avant-garde art through the celebrated Armoury Show for whom the spiritual discourse was quite in sync with modernism itself!

Modernist affinities between Coomaraswamy and the leading modernists who espoused formalism, such as Roger Fry and Clive Bell as a site of convergence between the art of the West and the East are queried by Allan Antliff. What started as a democratization of art at least from the point of view of reception according to Clive Bell — formalism only required one to have a healthy pair of eyes to understand art — became increasingly rarefied and lapsed into elitist aestheticism which was vigorously critiqued by Coomaraswamy. For Coomaraswamy, the social function of art and its cultural specificity are the terms through which modernist affinities could legitimately enter any discourse on East–West comparativism. Such a critique offered by Coomaraswamy is significant given the fact that when art history entered into the curriculum of Indian universities under the aegis of colonialism, it was formalism that was the dominant method adopted by art historians in India.

Deborah Jenner brings to light Coomaraswamy's impact on Georgia O'Keeffe's engagement with spirituality. It is not enough to point out that Coomaraswamy impacted both Georgia O'Keeffe and Alice Boner. It is necessary to grasp that despite their espousal of transcendence inspired by Coomaraswamy, their takes on it were very much centred around the body; it is through dancing and sketching that Boner reinterprets formal metaphysics just as O'Keeffe in her paintings of plants and flowers animates the conventional genre of still life and makes them pulsate with erotic spirituality. The symbolism of *yoni* (female vulva) and the phallic pillar intertwine in their ascent into the cosmic oneness through the Door in the sky. By seeing a structure of cosmic unity in a flower, O'Keeffe brings about an aesthetic shock or *samavega* that shatter the standard hierarchy between the secular and the sacred worlds.

Remarkable from the present perspective is the ease with which Coomaraswamy could deploy terms from Sanskrit aesthetics to capture what appears to be his reception of Stieglitz photographs almost as sublime. He brought into circulation a Sanskrit term — *samavega* and translated it as aesthetic shock. Even if this term does not get any validity from classical Sanskrit aesthetics, Coomaraswamy's move to deploy this term appears most radical! Today many art historians practising in the non-West are accused of being too reliant on Western terminologies and tools of discourse.

Sarah Turner looks at India Society in Britain as a site for a cultural encounter between India and the West within asymmetrical relations of power and imperialism. So far, Coomaraswamy's defence of Indian art has been understood primarily through his appeal to Indian iconography and the religious subject matter but Turner underlines how Coomaraswamy countered European misrepresentation of Indian art via modernist arguments invoking even the futurists' use of movement and this explains modernist sculptors such as Eric Gills' attraction towards Indian sculpture.

The faces of Coomaraswamy, the traditionalist and the modernist and the contemporary interpretative desire to revisit early the twentieth century opens up the history of modernism in a new way and perhaps it allows us to claim with Sarah Turner that British modernism did not emerge in splendid isolation, nor did it emerge in United States in any pristine purity. The art of the East began to so resonate with spiritual ethos that many a modernist was compelled to engage with it, each located within modernist media of photography, painting and sculpture. In fact, the concerns with the spiritual shaped modernism at its very inception — a perception that is gaining ground more in our times than in the heydays of modernism. Was the realm of the sacred present at the heart of modernism albeit in a repressed form? What does it reveal about our own times that we are prepared to rehabilitate Coomaraswamy's anti-modernism or his specific construct about modernism as a part of its larger story?

Now I will deal briefly with the views of the second panel.

As we step into the decades of the twenty-first century, the twentieth century acquires cohesiveness with a beginning and an end. As our glance travels backwards with our feet firmly in the present, the very history of the twentieth century art calls for a reassessment. While we move closer to the idea of global art history on one hand and the apocalyptic imagination of the end of art history, on the other, it is through these twin lens drawn from our contemporary preoccupations that early moments of modernism can be reconfigured. Is globalism a thing of the present or was it implicit at the inception of modernism itself? Wasn't the United States a haven where intellectuals from Europe and different parts of the world gravitated towards around the outbreak of First World War? Seen from this perspective, modernism can be seen less as an insular development localized to a region and more as exchange of ideas between the East and the West even if imperialism made the conditions of this exchange asymmetrical. The standard history of modernism attached high value to the entry of primitivism when we are asked to imagine Picasso's foray into Cubism without his exposure to the African wooden masks. The flipside of primitivism appears to be spiritualism, in which most diatribes against modernism seem to be couched. Coomaraswamy's towering presence in the early decades of the twentieth century amidst debates about the authenticity of modern art attests to this repressed trajectory of spiritualism. The more familiar construct of spiritualism is associated with some Western artists like Kandinsky who turned to non-Western sources to revitalize Western art. What sets Coomaraswamy apart is his being an "Indian" thinker who represented Indian philosophical thought via his notion of perennial philosophy and his claim to be an authentic spokesperson of the East. As a curator of the Indian section of the Boston Museum, he did not remain confined to traditional Indian art but through his practice of photography and friendship with Stieglitz and his circle, extended his role as a saviour of Asian art to a pioneering exponent of photography as an avant-garde artform.

For a champion of Eastern spiritualism who pitted it against Western materialism, the role of collecting was too much allied with the latter, as pointed out by Brinda Kumar. What further creates a dilemma for Coomaraswamy is the tension between the art historical functionality that constitutes the canon by placing art works within history and his a priori commitment to the timeless essence of Indian art that seeks synchronistic unity amongst the works. As has already been underlined in the earlier panel on Coomaraswamy, neither his espousal of perennial philosophy, nor his celebration of traditionalism posed any impediment to Coomaraswamy's pioneering recognition of photography as a legitimate artform. This may appear anomalous to us today but Lauren Kroiz shows a link in the most unexpected terrain — the realm of craft whose mechanical repetitiveness finds an equivalent in the mechanical objectivity of photography. What to a modernist theorist like Clement Greenberg was detrimental to any craft object seeking an avant-garde status was precisely what made photography "a living art form", according to Coomaraswamy. In this respect, Allan Sekulla's dismissal of Stieglitz as bringing about a closure through mystification of photography is questioned by Lauren against the light of Coomaraswamy's strategic use of spiritualism to accord aesthetic status to photography. What is highlighted in *How Ananda Coomaraswamy Made Modernist Photography a Spiritual Art* is the dual role of Coomaraswamy as a theorist and practitioner of photography.

Spiritualism and primitivism confront each other in the comparison made by Madhuri Desai between Coomaraswamy and Mircea Eliade. Exploring the professional and personal relationship between the champion of Indian art and that of comparative religion, Madhuri raises the larger question about what kind of universalism of art and religion may emerge out of the colonial conditions of knowledge production. If Eliade is seen as a cultural ethnographer in his encounter with the colonized East, Coomaraswamy strikes as a cultural insider at one level. However, it is when we consider the extent of convergence between their views around the East placed outside history, that reliance of Coomaraswamy on Eurocentric frameworks complicates his claims of being a cultural insider. Revisiting their writings, Madhuri queries the moment when the notion of timeless India got naturalized and became the common sense view about pre-modern Indian art.

All the three papers bring into sharp juxtaposition multiple roles played by Coomaraswamy as a curator, collector, ideologue and photographer. And what acts as a connecting link between these roles is the privileging of craft that applies as much to an art object made by a traditional craftsman as to the task of photographer. Long before Walter Benjamin exalted photography as mechanical reproduction, hence a tool for social and political transformation, Coomaraswamy invoked the repetitious act of craft and thereby its deployment of common semiotics, or, in his words, symbols so that both photography and traditional art practices received a moral and ethical endorsement. He seems to have been drawn to photography as an objective and mechanical medium that leaves little room for self-expression and hence is an ideal site for self-noughting, one of his favourite tropes. What he wanted the Western audience to learn from traditional Indian art — the ethics of selfless creativity and collective reflection — was already built into the apparatus of photography and its technology. He replaced the empirical dimension of photographic representation with spiritual vision — the place of archetypes and collective social imagination.

Coomaraswamy in the Globalized World

I have attempted an overview of a critical historiography of Coomaraswamy's writings across different moments from the 1970s to the present. In the centenary volume, some critical voices could be heard that brought out his discomfort with modernism and sensuous aesthetics, and his construct of traditional Indian art as largely transcendental and anti-mimetic remained normative. It was after a close reading of his interpretation of Sanskrit texts that the tendentious nature of his hermeneutics came to light and along with that were revealed earlier voices of dissent by V. Raghavan and Priyabala Shah.

On the other hand, around the turn of the twenty-first century, Euro-American scholarship revisited the legacy of Coomaraswamy and resurrected a new image of him as an ardent exponent of modernism. What drove this radical new take on Coomaraswamy's work? Perhaps the answer lies in our increasingly global world that has discovered multiplicity of cultures and plural modernisms in different parts of the world. This acknowledgement of cultural difference urged Western scholars to revisit early sites of modernism only to discover the multicultural figure of A.K. Coomaraswamy whose cultural hybridity equipped him to make equal claims of cultural relativism as well as perennial philosophy — to find in this visionary a delicate balance between universalism and cultural difference.

References

Coomaraswamy, A.K., "Viṣṇudharmottra Chapter XLI", *Journal of American Oriental Society*, **52**, 1932, pp. 13-21.

———, "The Painter's Art in Ancient India: Ajanta", *Journal of the Indian Society of Oriental Art*, **1**, 1933.

———, *The Transformation of Nature in Art*, New York: Dover, 1957.

Kapur, Geeta, "On the Vocation of the Artist", in *Parokṣa: Coomaraswamy*

Centenary Seminar Papers, ed. Gulam Mohammed Sheikh et al., New Delhi: Lalit Kala Akademi, 1984, pp. 148-51.

Kramrisch, Stella, "A Treatise on Indian Painting", *Journal of Department of Letters*, **2**(1924), pp. 1-56.

Raghavan, V., "Some Sanskrit Texts on Painting", *Journal of Indian Historical Quarterly*, 9, 1933, pp. 898-911.

Subramanyan, K.G., "The Significance of Coomaraswamy's Ideas in Our Times", in *Parokṣa: Coomaraswamy Centenary Seminar Papers*, ed. Gulam Mohammed Sheikh et al., New Delhi: Lalit Kala Akademi, 1984, pp. 16-17.

3

Aestheticizing the Nation
An Essay on Ananda Coomaraswamy

Mohan Ramanan

ANANDA Coomaraswamy's work needs to be studied in the context of Nationalist discourse. He is part of a group of remarkable nationalists — Tagore, Gandhi and Radhakrishnan to mention the more prominent — who conceived of the nation in several ways but still had a fundamental unity of purpose. Tagore, a friend of Coomaraswamy, had profound differences with Gandhi, precisely on the role played by art in society and the national life. Eschewing any narrow ideas of nationhood, he made common cause with Coomaraswamy in speaking of the local and the global, home and abroad, East and West, and of the national and the international as complementing one another and illuminating each other. Coomaraswamy, for example, says that to understand the nation one must understand internationalism. Tagore's position is fundamentally similar. Gandhi, on the other hand, was utilitarian in his conception of art and would not countenance anything which smacked of hedonism or beauty for its own sake. In this he was close to an art critic like John Ruskin whose *Unto This Last* influenced him greatly. Gandhi, in other words, was for duty, while Tagore, and one might add Coomaraswamy, were for beauty. Radhakrishnan brought a deep understanding of philosophy, both Eastern and Western, into play and he conceived of a national culture which would have the spirit of Vedantic universalism, a universalism which could not possibly have any truck with narrow domestic walls of insularity and xenophobia. Coomaraswamy would heartily agree. Both were against all forms of insensitivity. Coomaraswamy shares with Radhakrishnan something of this acceptance of universals and he is persuaded that Indian art is nothing if not universal in this sense because of its capacity for transcendence.

Coomaraswamy's work has also to be seen in the context of the cultural imperialism, embodied by British rule, which he was up against. He reacted to statements like the following from George Birdwood in his book on the industrial arts of India where Birdwood asserted:

> The monstrous shapes of the Puranic deities are unsuitable for the higher forms of artistic representation and this is possibly why sculptures and paintings are unknown as fine arts in India. — quoted in Jagmohan 1979: 36

Ruskin, for example, had this to say about Hindu art:

> If Indian art represents any living creature, it represents that creature in some distorted and monstrous form. To all the facts and forms of nature, it willfully and regularly opposes itself. — quoted ibid.

Vincent Smith, an early authority on Indian art, commented as follows:

> The many-headed, many-armed gods and goddesses whose images crowd the walls and roofs of medieval temples have no pretensions to beauty and are frequently hideous and grotesque. — quoted ibid.

Clearly this kind of prejudice was also the result of British ruling-class attitudes. Colonialism bolstered cultural imperialism. It had to be countered and Ananda Coomaraswamy made it his life's mission to do just that. In the process he upheld the national ideal but not in any xenophobic manner.

In his essay, which gives the title to the book *The Dance of Shiva*, Coomaraswamy, after giving a brilliant exposition of the symbolism of the Naṭarāja figure by linking the image to the concept, the visual appeal to the ideological, states that this icon is representative of the essence of Indian art. It is about the all-pervading nature of the Supreme Being who is immanent and pervasive and who evokes nothing less than an universal appeal. While Coomaraswamy believes that this is essentially Indian, he has no narrow conception of Indianness because in his scheme of things, the nation is part of the international. It is this catholicity in Coomaraswamy which is the burden of this paper and I have no hesitation in saying that this is what India is all about — at least the India of the great national leaders who contributed so much to the conception of an imagined community in the early years of the twentieth century. This paper attempts, therefore, to explore the symbiotic manner in which Coomaraswamy's thought moves from national pride to a conception of art and the consequent aestheticizing of the nation. That contribution fuses with the overtly political and philosophical contributions of Gandhi, Tagore and Radhakrishnan, not to speak of Swami Vivekananda, Bankim Chandra, Keshub Chandra Sen, Sri Aurobindo — all of whom one might join together as thinkers who promoted the spiritual dimensions of Indian nationalism.

Coomaraswamy's love for India was lifelong and in fact he was contemplating retirement from his duties at the Boston Museum and settling down in the northern hills of the imagined nation of his dreams. Coomaraswamy travelled all over India in search of the quintessence of our culture. He not only collected large treasure troves of art and literature, but interpreted them and translated them for an international audience. He was no textbook critic. He actually sought out the descendants of India's traditional artisans and studied their lives and culture because he believed that the arts are the outward reflection of deep structures of lived experience. He saw art in its totality, not just as artefacts but as communiqués, both as things made and as things said. He believed in the unity of art and life and society and sought the essence of India in her art. He was compelled to do this because of his encounter with colonialism. British colonialism affected not just India but his native Ceylon (now Sri Lanka) and he saw the effects of that rule in the deracination of the people who were aping Western mores and dress and food styles, to the detriment of home-grown things. Added to this was the unmistakable prejudice of the West about things Indian as we have seen from the quotations I have given of Birdwood, Ruskin and others.

The Western critics saw our art as barbaric, grotesque and fantastic. Coomaraswamy bristling with national pride refuted these charges, not through any irritable reaching out to atavistic energies or primitive knee-jerk responses but through a considered and informed analysis of the meaning and symbolism of our art. He saw what Sussane Langer has called "significant form" in our sculptures and for the first time, the West, in a language it understood, was enlightened about the nature of the Buddha figures, which according to Coomaraswamy were not of Greek origins as a critic like Boucher believed, but Gāndhāra. He also distinguished between Mughal and Kāṅgṛā art, something conflated by Western critics. He established the framework by which Indian art would be studied for generations. He was a stupendous scholar who wrote indefatigably about his passion. Ironically the country that he loved did not want him and he went away to Boston where he flourished. One could speculate as to whether distance lends enchantment to the view and leads to misinterpretation but in Coomaraswamy's case this distance gave him the necessary objectivity and detachment to speak of Indian art with great authority backed by irrefutable evidence of scholarship. There is a rare passion in utterances born of detachment and Coomaraswamy's animated speculations are informed by that quality.

Romain Rolland introducing Coomaraswamy's excellent collection of essays *The Dance of Shiva* commented that the author was a brāhmaṇa seer and that he himself had been swept away by "the powerful rhythm of Brahmin thought" (Coomaraswamy 1982: 8) and returning to his Einsteinian universe he found it not strange at all because the new cosmogony was in compliance with the laws of the spirit and he could hear "resounding still the cosmic symphony of all the planets, which forever succeed each other, are extinguished and once more illumined, with their living souls, their humanities, their gods — according to the law of the eternal to become, the brāhmaṇa *saṁsāra* — I hear Śiva dancing, dancing in the heart of the world, in my own heart" (1982: 9).

The universality of Coomaraswamy's Brāhmanical thought is Rolland's burden and indeed when one turns to the essay which eponymously gives the volume its title we are confirmed in this view by Coomaraswamy himself addressing this issue of universality. He has spent a few pages lovingly describing the magnificent iconic significance of the Naṭarāja idol and in conclusion says that he has "endeavoured to translate the central thought of the conception of Śiva's dance from plastic to verbal expression, without reference to the beauty or imperfection of individual works" (ibid: 93).

But what is remarkable about this icon is essentially evocative of the idea of India — it is her capacity for synthesis of science, religion and art. And this is what Coomaraswamy claims:

> How amazing the range of thought and sympathy of those *ṛṣi*-artists who first conceived such a type as this, affording an image of reality, a key to the complex tissue of life, a

> theory of nature, not merely satisfactory to a single clique or race, nor acceptable to the thinkers of one century only, but universal in its appeal to the philosopher, the lover, and the artist of all ages and all countries. How supremely great in power and grace this dancing image must appear to all those who have striven in plastic forms to give expression to their intuition of Life. — ibid.: 93-94

This is a remarkable statement because it not only suggests that Brāhmanical thought was universal but that it was essentially Indian. It is not the kind of perception which will be appreciated today in our times of stress and identity politics but we must read Coomaraswamy in his context, some of which I have already sketched. Coomaraswamy is saying this in a specific time and place and he is doing it in order to emphasize for unsympathetic Westerners, the greatness of the culture to which he is a heir, to stress that in relation to Western dualities, India stressed the unity and synthetic power of the imagination. It is also an attempt to distinguish what is distinctive about India. But he does not stop with this because he posits a timelessness for that culture which of course for us in Pocomo (post-colonial, post-modern) times is problematic. Coomaraswamy adds:

> Every part of such an image as this is directly expressive, not of any mere superstition or dogma, but of evident facts. No artist of today, however great, could more exactly or more wisely create an image of that Energy which science must postulate behind all phenomena. If we would reconcile Time with Eternity, we can scarcely do so otherwise than by the conception of alternations of phase extending over vast regions of space and great tracts of time. Especially significant, then, is the phase alternation implied by the drum, and the fire which changes, not destroys. These are but visual symbols of the theory of the day and night of Brahmā. — ibid.: 94

Rolland points to the organicity of such icons and Coomaraswamy makes an implicit connection between organicity of art and organicity of society. He believed that India had such a cultural formation and that this was not different from the organicity of art and society in pre-industrial Europe, of Medieval Europe or Christendom, to be specific. Incidentally such a view is propounded by Sri Aurobindo also in *Foundations of Indian Culture*. The belief that in a world of organic integrity, artists are like kings, is a view Coomaraswamy shares with many contemporaries. One of them is W.B. Yeats whose Byzantium represents the zenith of artistic and societal perfection. Such a belief in an organic world perhaps has no basis in fact or in historical terms and we have Raymond William's critique of the Leavisian notion of organicity in *The Country and the City*. But as Frank Kermode has pointed out, if an organic society did not exist it would need to be invented, because it is a psychological necessity. It is a belief, Yeats and his fellow Modernist poets, T.S. Eliot and Ezra Pound, in their various ways held, as did Gandhi who shared an affinity in this respect with William Morris and John Ruskin. Now one understands that such a view helps a thinker to make sense of his present condition and clearly Coomaraswamy was motivated by his sense of colonial humiliation to posit such an Indian Golden Age. As far as we are concerned, such a view helped India to feel some pride in herself and whether such a Golden Age existed or not, it helped Indians to take their place in the comity of nations and to get the West to take notice.

Coomaraswamy's organic theory also suggests that he is a traditionalist and his view of art is emphatic in its stress on universal values. It also, as we have seen, is a combination of art, life and culture, a combination Coomaraswamy implicitly advances. That is why he is able to speak of Asia's primary role in civilization. Asia (read India) has given the world lessons in organicity and synthesis, where opposites dissolve and fuse into a unity. Tagore's idea of East–West rapprochement is Coomaraswamy's too, but it is not the West of materialism, of modern democracy and of Industrial capitalism which Coomaraswamy has in mind. He is aligned to the West in its culture of Christendom where the artisans were a part of a guild and formed a socialistic pattern of community living. Morrisian guild socialism was practised in India and Coomaraswamy, it must be remembered, had close connections with Morris's printing press and was influenced by his ideas. Indeed there is a tradition of nineteenth-century acceptance of guild culture and the most prominent figures in this are Ruskin, Morris, Carpenter and on the Indian side, I believe, Gandhi, if one goes by some of his pronouncements, and of course Coomaraswamy. It is of the same vintage as those who believe that there was a time in history when people felt their thought and thought their feelings, creating art through the exercise of a unified sensibility. That modern capitalism and industrialization is the cause for a dissociation of sensibility is accepted by Gandhi and Coomaraswamy, not to speak of Sri Aurobindo who in *Foundations of Indian Culture* speaks eloquently of the fundamental convergence of medieval European and Indian arts.

Coomaraswamy says that Indian art is able to see the one in the many and this is because India can keep faith when all is said and done and overcome the sheer weight of laziness and sloth and modernist prejudice and assert its message. India has done so for centuries and Coomaraswamy believes that she can do so in the future, provided interpreters like him can assert their criticism in the face of colonialism. Time for India is cosmic, not the contingent and the quotidian, and her art correspondingly has no truck with photographic realism but asserts the morphology of divinity in the midst of myriad forms. India can show stillness in the midst of activity, the stillness of the dancing Śiva. This is her philosophy and this is how, as Rolland points out, philosophy has been applied to social living. Indian art is differentiated by its capacity to suggest still action. The West has known only rapacious and predatory action after it lost its soul to capitalism and colonialism.

Coomaraswamy also develops a view of social organization as a result of his belief in the organicity of things. Man is born with a purpose in life and his quest is not self-gratification but the fulfilment of his destiny. Coomaraswamy is able to see the complex phenomenon of caste in these terms as something which facilitates the individual in fulfilling his destiny. The purpose is both individual salvation in *dharma* and also the assertion of a *dharma* which, to put it in his own words, is to build a city of the gods. Philosophy in this quest is a means, never an end as it has become in the West. His is a critique of materialism and an assertion of the *dharma* of man and of society. He is enthused by the example of the ancient Brāhmanical civilization which learnt to apply religious philosophy to the problems of sociology. Religion was quite clearly the basis for culture, a view which Eliot and Matthew Arnold would share. In Coomaraswamy's scheme of things the material was suffused with the spiritual and the spiritual included the material. Both coexisted in a synthesis. This is visible in the fourfold purpose of life in Hindu thought where the good life is described as the pursuit of the ends of *dharma*, *artha*, *kāma* and *mokṣa*. One's life has to be framed by righteousness, and the economic and the instinctual life must be informed by *dharma* so that the final end of man may be attained, which is *mokṣa*. In this scheme of *puruṣārtha*s, the world is not negated but *dharma* suffuses the world with its potent spirit. The world is never too much with us because we are the world but we can make a heaven of the world by living life well.

This leads to great tolerance and acceptance. Nothing is excluded because there is in the Brāhmanical doctrine space for everything, every nuance and every mode. However, this does not preclude a premium being placed on excellence and on a hierarchy of intellect. Clearly Coomaraswamy is close to Blake with his idea of the prolifics and Nietszche Friedrich Wilhelm, with his idea of the masters. He is promoting an aristocracy of the intellect and the true communion of minds which in their higher states will exemplify a standard of conduct. The Hindu view of tāmasic, rājasic and sāttvic individuals is of course apropos. It is an elitist view, not likely to find favour in our days of equalitarianism, but it is inspiring to see how an important strain in Indian thought found in the modern period a great and eloquent articulator and how one man could conceive of a national character by combining philosophy, literature, art and religion to produce an aesthetic idea of the nation. It is the exact opposite of the modern industrial society. It has little to do with competition but everything to do with co-operation. This is the unified sensibility of an Indian society which for Coomaraswamy existed between the fourth and the eighth century, the golden age of Indian civilization. It is an age where art was *yoga* and set its face against the hedonism which passes for art. For Coomaraswamy, civilization in its etymological dimension is nothing other than a city, a *pura*, where the *Puruṣa* (God) resides. God alone is the citizen. The sun is the *sūtra* (string) of unity which threads the diverse strands into an organic whole. The ideal society is a co-operative and work here is carried out in a spirit of detachment because work is everyone's *svadharma*.

What makes art have the quality Coomaraswamy attributes to it? For him it is *vyañjanā* or *rasa* with its determinants, consequents, *bhāva*s and *sattvabhāva*s. This makes art experience centrally a question of evoking the *rasa*s. Art itself is *rasavanta* and the reader enjoying the *rasa* is a *rasika*. This in turn makes the experience *rasāsvādana*. This is equivalent to *brahmānanda*. It is a transcendent experience we are talking about because art experience takes one beyond good and evil. A *rasika* beholds beauty and reacts in his own way but his responsive imagination (*bhāvayitrī pratibhā*) differs from that of the creative imagination (*kāvayitrī pratibhā*) of the artist only in degree not in kind. Both *rasika* and *kavi* are subsumed under the category of God who in Coleridge's terms is the author of the primary imagination, the first creator.

Coomaraswamy has a book called *Essays in National Idealism*. It is about the manner in which national character has been destroyed by the West and by the so-called civilizing mission of imperialism. We have no pride in ourselves and we are a pale imitation of the West. As a Ceylonese Tamil he was interested in a Ceylonese renaissance, and because he saw Ceylon as symbiotically connected to the Indian subcontinent, he was interested in an Indian renaissance as well. In art culture he was close to the Śāntiniketan painters like Abanindranath Tagore and Nandlal Bose, and spoke of their work approvingly. He promoted local arts and crafts and he had hands on experience of this activity because, as we noted earlier, he not only collected artefacts but traced the families which traditionally practised the craft, and wrote about their lives and culture. In other words, art was firmly a social thing and the national spirit was always reflected in art. Like Carpenter, Morris and Ruskin, he too was against industrial civilization and opposed that with his emphasis on local guilds and crafts. He was a guild socialist like Morris and his views are in consonance with Sri Aurobindo, Tagore and Gandhi — all of whom in their writings critiqued Western industrial civilization. He also saw industrialism as the hand maiden of colonialism and imperialism, and his criticism was therefore anticolonial. But in the process, like Tagore, he was also able to see beyond narrow domestic walls and speak of an international culture. That is because the culture of the arts knows no boundaries. The whole world is its space and as the ancient Sanskrit saying goes, it is *vasudhaiva kuṭumbakam*. Nations are made by artists. This is what I mean by asserting that Coomaraswamy in his writings is aestheticizing the nation.

Coomaraswamy was not unaware of the *swadeshi* spirit the Extremists in Congress had promoted after the Moderate consensus broke down in the first decade of the twentieth century. He speaks of art as having much to do with *swadeshi* but he had his reservations about the burning of foreign cloth and the boycott of foreign goods. These activities were wasteful and would not resuscitate a nation if the people did nothing to preserve and promote the local crafts and arts. While agreeing with Gandhi about the need to get away from mechanical machine culture and sharing his Luddite views, Coomaraswamy was not averse to using technology in the service of art. He was for the preservation of the variety of local and specific traditions which were in danger of being subsumed by the uniformity of industrialization. But here Gandhi and Coomaraswamy part. The former is not aesthetic at all in his views but the latter is an aesthetic saint.

Coomaraswamy believed that Buddhist and Hindu art forms were symbiotic and mutually intertwined and the burden of his essays in the *Dance of Shiva* is to the effect that the two cannot be separated. In fact, he believes, as we noted, that the origins of Buddhist art have to be seen in Gandhara art and not, as Boucher believed, in Greek culture. This, at that time an astonishing claim, is now borne out, and Coomaraswamy established the criterion by which art could be studied in general and Buddhism in particular. Swami Vivekananda's claim that Vedānta and Buddhism are not in competition, but are complementary, is borne out by the resonance of Coomaraswamy's claims. By establishing the Hindu context of Buddhist art, Coomaraswamy erected a formidable defence against cultural imperialism and the civilizational disdain we noted earlier. Coomaraswamy, like Tagore, asked for a national education which would free us from mental slavery and give a fitting answer to the likes of Ruskin and other prejudiced thinkers.

Coomaraswamy, then, goes to the essence of things and interprets the essence of India through her art and the philosophy it embodies. His trajectory, as someone pointed out, is from art to philosophy, the perennial philosophy which so enthused people like Aldous Huxley. As a polyhistorian and a polyglot, Coomaraswamy was able to compare several linguistic and art traditions to see what was common in them and his syncretic approach was part of his internationalism. From this he is able to derive a "common universe of discourse" and stress the transcendental values which people of different persuasions like Schweitzer, Russell, Rolland and Tagore held dear. For him, then, tradition is not a thing of the past. It is the pastness of the past in the present, and this Eliotic dimension allowed him to live in the present like a *ṛṣi*. Did that make him less modern as some would have it? I think not. He would have retired to India to the Himalayas for his traditional *vānaprastha* but death overcame him. Gandhi's *satya* and *ahiṁsā* appealed to him and he was for making peace with society, but his medium for doing so was art. He was anti-Cartesian and reversed Descartes by stating — "That I Think is proof that Thou Art". For him art was a symbol of an entire approach to the business of living. That is why in his works he stressed the connection between the nation, its ideals, transcendence and aesthetics. He wrote:

> May I know and become what I am, no longer this man, so and so, but the Self that is also the Being of all beings, my Self and your Self. — Jagmohan 1979: 97

This statement sums up the philosophical basis of Coomaraswamy's aesthetics and since this is a Vedāntic thought, it pretty much sums up for us the connection between art, philosophy and the Indian nation.

References

Coomaraswamy, Ananda, 1982, *The Dance of Shiva*, with an Introductory Preface by Romain Rolland, New Delhi: Munshiram Manoharlal.

Jagmohan, 1979, *Ananda K. Coomaraswamy*, New Delhi: Publication Division, Ministry of Information and Broadcasting, Government of India.

4

Polemics of Decolonization
The Art Criticism of Sri Aurobindo and Ananda Coomaraswamy

Sachidananda Mohanty

I

SHORTLY after August 1910, on exile from British India at the French enclave of Pondicherry, Sri Aurobindo wrote a rejoinder to an article entitled "Comment and Criticism: The Indian Fine Arts Critics", earlier published in *The Modern Review* of Calcutta (**8**(2): 207-13). The *Review's* editor identified the author of the article as "a student of Ravi Varma (1848–1906) the famous Indian artist". While defending Varma, the article made disparaging remarks against critics such as Ananda K. Coomaraswamy and Sister Nivedita.

Castigating the reviewer for his "theatrical wit and schoolboy impertinence", Sri Aurobindo thought that "the Ravi Varma superstition in India had received its quietus". For the painter in question, "is the grand debaser of Indian taste and artistic culture". Sadly, "a belated lance is lifted in the August number of *The Modern Review* for the fallen idol" (2003: 468).

The hostility displayed in the review, adds Sri Aurobindo, is baffling. After all, he says:

> Dr. Coomaraswamy is a critic of established reputation whose contributions to the study of Indian Art are valued in every country in Europe and Asia where the subject is

> studied. Sister Nivedita's literary genius, exquisite sympathetic insights and fine artistic culture are acknowledged by all who have the faculty of judging both in England and in India. Havell has a recognized position in the criticism of art. One may differ from such authorities, but one is at least bound to treat them with some show of respect. — Sri Aurobindo 2003: 468-69

While the criticism towards Nivedita and Havell are somewhat guarded, possibly because they are foreigners, Coomaraswamy's credentials, Sri Aurobindo suggests, are dismissed by referring to him, as a "geologist" and a "doctor". The idea apparently is to project the Indian art critic as an imposter. There is the display of a "characteristic specimen of wit" in the *Modern Review*:

> We cannot expect anything better from a geologist, who naturally loves and is made to love everything rigid and stony. — Ibid. 469

The text of Sri Aurobindo's rejoinder was incomplete and the piece remained unpublished during his lifetime. However, its contents are worthy of critical attention since the contents are in line with much of what he wrote on the subject around this time. It illuminates our understanding of several issues of the day and draws attention to unresolved questions of post-coloniality, and contemporary cultural criticism. These include our understanding of the relationship between traditions and modernities, usable traditions and unusable modernities, religious nationalism and secular modernity, cultural continuities/universals *vis-à-vis* cultural specifics, and finally, the "mission" and "uniqueness" of cultures vs. cultures seen as socio-historical and political constructs.

While I shall allude to some of the above during the course of my essay, I shall primarily focus on the role of the arts in the polemics of decolonization used by two kindred spirits of the early twentieth century; namely Sri Aurobindo and Coomaraswamy.

While post-colonial critics such as Edward Said, Homi Bhabha, Gayatri Spivak and Aizaz Ahmed have unveiled the colonial cartography in ample measure, there seems to be a surprising omission of the earlier narratives of decolonization during the early part of the twentieth century. Many of these seem to belong to the dominant religious/spiritual traditions of the day. Later and more recent approaches have preferred the secular and cultural materialist position. Modern systems of thought have not paid adequate attention to the question of faith and the notion of the sacred. The upsurge in religious fundamentalism worldwide could be one of the many factors that may have caused an intellectual wariness when handling this question. I shall argue in this essay that there is a need to come up with an alternative theory. For, the omission has impoverished post-colonial theory significantly. It has ignored a vital world-view and a significant part of the cultural history of South Asia. For my purpose, I shall take up for closer study the art criticism of Ananda Coomaraswamy and Sri Aurobindo against the backdrop of decolonization that was central to both the figures.

II

There are remarkable parallels (and notable differences) between Sri Aurobindo (15 August 1872 – 5 December 1950) and Coomaraswamy (22 August 1877 – 9 September 1947). Their lifespan makes them contemporaries. Both came from upper class/caste backgrounds and both were products of the modern West. Coomaraswamy's parents were the Ceylonese Tamil legislator and philosopher Sir Muthu Coomaraswamy and his English wife Elizabeth Beeby who denied him maternal affection. Young Coomaraswamy lost his father at the age of two and was educated and brought up abroad. Moving to England in 1879, at the age of 12, he attended a preparatory school in Stround, Gloucestershire and graduated from University College, London, in 1900 with a degree in Geology and Botany.

On 19 June 1902, Coomaraswamy married Ethel Mary Partridge and moved to Ceylon. His contributions to mineralogy led to the formation of the Geological Survey of Ceylon which he headed for some time.

After his divorce and second marriage to an English woman who performed on stage under the name of Ratan Devi, he moved to the United States to serve as the first keeper of Indian Art in the Museum of Fine Arts in Boston in 1917. He had two more marriages, to American artist Stella Bloch in November 1922 and Argentine Luisa Runstein in November 1930. He was a distinguished member of the art circle in New York City, and a close friend of the artist Alfred Stieglitz. In 1933 he became a Fellow for Research in Indian, Persian and Mohammedan Art at the Museum of Fine Arts.

He wrote more than thirty books on art, sculpture, art history, architecture, philosophy, metaphysics and East–West relations, and undoubtedly ranks as one of the best known exponents of Indian arts in the West. His middle name "Kentish", marker of a valorized English pedigree and culture, generally unnoticed in his later career, might signify a dethronement of one's colonial past. Both in his life and vocations, he stands at the crossroads between tradition and modernity, the East and the West. He stood for values described as inalienably "Indian" and yet chose places of work outside India and life companions who were not Indian, who some could say went beyond national boundaries and political frontiers. He was synthetic and universal in outlook. Part of the close circle of Rabindranath Tagore, he chose the art galleries and museums of the advanced West as his places of work and for the dissemination of ideas. His many lives flowed effortlessly from nationalism to cosmopolitanism, based on the primacy of the arts. From the English soil he seems to draw sustenance from Victorian critics like Mathew Arnold, John Ruskin and Dante Gabriel Rossetti with the latter's faith in the centrality of art in Victorian Society. There are also the influences of the earlier historical periods such as the Hellenic, the European Renaissance and other civilization of the world such as the ancient, pre-colonial India that underlined the importance of the arts and aesthetics in national life. Blake's vision of a new Hellas or a New Jerusalem that marks the fusion between art and the New World would be a favoured ideal for Coomaraswamy.

Coomaraswamy's ideas, beliefs and life values, both artistic and creative, were not derivative. He assimilated influences both old and new, and forged approaches that were innovative and creative.

III

Coomaraswamy's better-known counterpart in this essay, Sri Aurobindo, had an equally anglicized upbringing and carried an English style middle name, "Akroyd", after his father's friend Annettle Akroyd, the founder of the Brahmo girls' school in Calcutta (cf. Heehs 1979: 7). Aurobindo's parents were Kristo Dhone Ghose (or K.D. Ghose) and Swarnalotta, daughter of Rajnarayan Basu, a leading member of the Brahmo Samaj and Bengal Renaissance. K.D. Ghose a doctor who earned a degree of MD from Aberdeen University, UK was thoroughly anglicized and wanted his children to follow in his footsteps. Like Coomaraswamy, Sri Aurobindo and his brothers, particularly Manmohan and Barindra Kumar were denied maternal affection. Soon after Aurobindo's birth, Swarnalotta showed signs of mental disorder which persisted till the end of her life.

At the Ghose household, no Indian languages including Bengali were spoken. The three children were admitted to the Loreto Convent, Darjeeling in 1877. Later in 1879, they were taken to Manchester and left under the care of a congregational minister named William H. Drewett who was asked by K.D. Ghose not to allow the children to "make the acquaintance of any Indian or undergo any Indian influence" (ibid.: 9). Although an agnostic, K.D. Ghose insisted that his children ought to be left free to decide about the question of faith. During his early years Aurobindo remained an agnostic. After spending five years at Manchester, Aurobindo studied at St. Paul's school, London in 1884 and King's College, Cambridge in 1890. In 1892 he passed the ICS but did not appear at a riding test and was disqualified.

Aurobindo arrived in Bombay (Mumbai) on 6 February 1893 and joined the Baroda Service, first in the administration and then as a Professor of English and French at the Baroda College. By 1900, he turned attention to the national freedom struggle. He established contact with secret societies in Maharashtra and Bengal. On 30 April 1902 he married Mrinalini Bose. He plunged actively into the *swadeshi* movement in 1905 over the partition of Bengal and became the editor of *Bande Mataram* in 1906. He joined as the Principal of Bengal National College. In 1908 he was arrested in the Alipore Bomb Case and after a year in jail he was acquitted on 6 May 1909. After his acquittal he edited two journals *Dharma* and *Karmayogin*. Following a divine command (*ādeśa*) he reached Pondicherry on 4 April 1910. On 29 March 1914 he met, Mirra Alfassa later known as the Mother who became his spiritual collaborator. From August 1914 to January 1921 the English monthly *Arya* carried his best-known writings. On 19 September 1940, during the Second World War, Sri Aurobindo declared support for Allies. He gave the Independence Day message on 15 August 1947 where he spelt out his vision of a new resurgent India and the future of humanity. Towards the end of his life, he devoted attention to his magnum opus, *Savitri*, and passed away on 5 December 1950.

I have spent some time in drawing attention to the key aspects of the life histories of the two figures because I believe the main trajectories of their lives have a bearing on the decolonizing agenda they championed.

Sri Aurobindo is widely known as a nationalist, philosopher and mystic. He looked at himself primarily as a poet. His reputation as a spiritual *guru* and saint has somewhat eclipsed his considerable body of critical and cultural writings, a portion of which deals significantly with literature and the arts. As in the case of Coomaraswamy, Sri Aurobindo's conceptions of art and his significant art criticism are to be seen as the inextricable part of his larger view of life, in which decolonization plays a crucial role. While the Ceylonese thinker's writings on art are better known than his views on and participation in the political struggle for freedom, Sri Aurobindo's nationalistic writings are better recognized than his art criticism. Even the more celebrated *The Foundations of Indian Culture* which appeared in the *Arya* from November 1918 to January 1921 and which contain a significant body of criticism devoted to sculpture, painting, music and architecture have not received the attention they deserve among students of art history and comparative aesthetics.

The chapter on Indian Art offers a comprehensive account on this subject. This and four other chapters gain significance from the opening chapter provocatively titled "Is India Civilized?". The underlying argument is that all aspects of national culture including the arts have to be seen against the backdrop of the Indian nationhood. The discovery of the meaning of the Indian nation against the then wealthier world civilizations is therefore an essential requisite for art criticism of both Coomaraswamy and Sri Aurobindo. There are at least three specific references to Coomaraswamy in the *Collected Works of Sri Aurobindo* (CWSA) (new edition), *Early Cultural Writings*, pp. 468-69, *Renaissance in India*, p. 255 and *Karmayogin*, pp. 244-48.

Coomaraswamy's best known work *The Dance of Shiva* was published by Sun Wise Turn Press, New York in 1918 around the time Sri Aurobindo published *The Renaissance in India*, August–November 1918. The equally notable art criticism of Sri Aurobindo comprised the period between 1909 and 1910 and all of them, namely *The National Value of Art*, a series of six essays, "Two Pictures", "Indian Art and an Old Classic" and "The Revival of Indian Art" appeared in the *Karmayogin*. Similarly two other essays in the form of reviews appeared in the *Arya*. "South Indian Bronzes" was published in the journal in October 1915 and in the *Views and Reviews* since 1941. Likewise, "Rupam" was published in the *Arya* in July 1917 and in the *Views and Reviews* since 1941. Since the journal *Arya* enjoyed a good circulation and was widely noticed in nationalistic, philosophical and cultural circles, it would be fair to assume that Coomaraswamy and Sri Aurobindo were broadly aware of each other's writings although we may not have enough knowledge regarding the actual correspondence between the two.

Aside from *The Foundations of Indian Culture* and *Early Cultural Writings*, Sri Aurobindo underlined his approach to decolonization in *The Secret of the Vedas* where he gave a symbolic interpretation of the Vedas from the Indian point of view.

IV

Let me consider Coomaraswamy's *The Dance of Shiva* from the points of my arguments implicit in the title of this paper. The book is divided into chapters that include, among others, the following: Indian Philosophy of Life, View of Art: Hindu and Buddhist, the Dance of Shiva, Status of Indian Women, Sahaja and Young India.

Each race, contends Coomaraswamy, contributes something unique to the world's civilizations in keeping with its own spirit, its own *svabhāva*. India's own contribution would be its Indianness. While there cannot be anything absolutely unique with regard to any nation's experience, "its peculiarities will be chiefly a matter of selection and emphasis, certainly not a difference in specific humanity (1918: 3).

India's genius, he says, is found in a "constant intuition of the unity of all life", and "the conviction that the recognition of this unity is the highest good and the uttermost freedom". This view has permeated all aspects of her life and is the essential basis of sociology and education. Along with this view, there are several other concepts that lend uniqueness to this approach. *Mokṣa* liberates us from *avidyā* (ignorance). It believes in the Will to Power rather than the Will to Life that characterizes the dominant commercialism of the modern West. Unlike the Hindu view, the Buddhist advocates an "escape from the eternal recurrence" as the *summum bonum*, the wisest purpose of life. There is the "religion of eternity" (*nirguṇa vidyā*) and the religion of time (*saguṇa vidyā*). The ideal is not to create a distinction between the sacred and the profane but "to illuminate daily life with the life of heaven".

Other categories are equally noteworthy: *pravṛtti mārga* typified by outward movement, the path of pursuit and self-assertion and *nivṛtti mārga*, the path of return and inward self-realization.

While this world-view preaches equality among men and women, there cannot be absolute equality, because as Coomaraswamy argues, "variation of temperament or inheritance . . . constitutes the natural inequality of men, an inequality that is too often ignored by the theories of Western democracies". India's social institutions including the marriage systems, he adds, have wisely emphasized duties rather than rights. Here again, as in the case of the caste system, Coomaraswamy seems to be less forthcoming about the pronounced inequity in the Indian society.

The character of the world process follows a rhythmic process; subject–object, self–non-self, will–matter, unity–diversity, love–hate, birth–death, evolution–involution, descent–ascent and *sṛṣṭi–saṁhāra.*

The *caturvarṇa* that is the basis of the Indian caste system, argues Coomaraswamy is "designed rather to unite than to divide". For the members of the different castes enjoy greater commonalities than differences. The system demands higher ethical and spiritual standards from the so-called upper castes. The higher the position in the caste hierarchy, the more stringent is the punishment for transgression. "For, responsibility rises with intelligence and status." We have here a body of collective privileges and responsibilities akin to guild socialism. There is unfortunately "decay" in Asia because of the shift from co-operation to competition. Such a turn may spell doom for Europe. It will not be able to fight industrialism because this enemy will be entrenched in Asia (cf. ibid.: 20). The objective of human life is not the pursuit of material life, physical objects and comforts, but to develop the "mental, moral and spiritual powers latent in man".

V

Sri Aurobindo's exposition of Indian culture, outlined in *The Foundations of Indian Culture*, was written in response to "an extravagant *jeu d'esprit*" by William Archer, the dramatic critic in his *India and the Future*. The latter volume was ably critiqued by John Woodroffe in a defence provocatively entitled *Is India Civilized?: Essays on Indian Culture*. The epigraph to Woodroffe's opening chapter is a telling quotation from Archer that sums up the latter's view of India:

> Barbarian, barbarism, barbarous — I am sorry to harp so much on these words. But they express the essence of the situation. . . . There are of course many thousands of individuals who have risen and are rising above it

> (barbarism), but the plain truth concerning the mass of the (Indian) population — and not the poorer classes alone — is that they are not civilized people.
>
> — quoted in Woodroffe 1919: 12

"How do we judge a culture?", asks Sri Aurobindo. "The greatness of a culture lies in the manner it tries to effect a 'natural harmony of spirit, mind and body'. Spirituality is the keynote of Indian culture although others have also had spiritual components to their own. All cultures go through the stages of conflict, competition, concert and finally the spirit of sacrifice and mutual sharing."

"We see the desire of Europe", argues Sri Aurobindo, "to Europeanize the entire world in its self-image. Either India will be rationalized or industrialized out of all recognition or will be 'the leader of a new phase' Indian Religion has passed through four principal stages. It comprises the following:

1. A belief in the highest conscious state of existence.
2. A need for self-preparation by development and experience.
3. An imperative to provide well-founded knowledge and self-discipline.
4. A necessity to sustain an organization of the individual and collective life for gradual progress."

While the *caturvarṇa* in its intention may have envisaged a flexible structure of the fourfold order, Sri Aurobindo is firm that the caste system of the later period was an utter caricature and ought to be discarded. He makes no compromises regarding systems he sees as outmoded and therefore must be cast off completely.

For the European mind there is the Indian "political incompetence", "despotism of the brāhmaṇa theocracy" and "absolute monarchy of the Oriental". In reality, however, the

Indian polity was based on communal freedom and self-discrimination.

As Sri Aurobindo wrote insightfully in August 1919 in the *Arya:*

> The mentality of the West has long cherished the aggressive and quite illogical idea of a single religion for all mankind, a religion universal by the very force of its narrowness, one set of dogma, one cult, one system of ceremonies, one array of prohibitions and injunctions, one ecclesiastical ordinance. That narrow absurdity prances about as the one true religion which all must accept on peril of persecution by men here and spiritual rejection or fierce, eternal punishment by god in other worlds. — 1993: 146

Both Sri Aurobindo and Coomaraswamy discarded a return to the past, to any form of revivalism, for the clock, they said, cannot be turned back. There is a paramount need for "creative introspection preparatory to renewed activity". "The first expression of national idealism is then a rehabilitation of the past" (Coomaraswamy 1918: 166). As he declares aptly:

> We would not and cannot return. In India, as in Europe, the vestige of ancient civilization must be renounced: we are called from the past and must make our home in the future. But to understand, to endorse with passionate conviction and to love what we have left behind us is the only possible foundation for power. If the time has hardly yet come for the creation of new values — and it cannot long be delayed — let us remember that time and sufferings are essential to all creation. — ibid.

Sri Aurobindo is equally futuristic in his approach while advocating a renewed understanding of our past. Writing in the *Arya* in May 1918 he outlined his vision of the future that clearly goes beyond nationalism and the project of decolonization of the Indian mind. It embraces his prophecy in the terrestrial evolution and the coming of a new spiritual society. He wrote:

> Man's road to spiritual Supermanhood will be open when he declares boldly that all he has yet developed, including the intellect of which he is so vainly proud, are now no longer sufficient for him. Light within shall be henceforth a pervading preoccupation. Then will this philosophy, art, science, ethics, social existence, vital pursuits be no longer an exercise in mind and life, done for themselves, carried in a circle, but a means of discovery of a greater truth behind mind and life and for the bringing of its power into our human existence. — 1997: 135

VI

What then is the conception of art here? Since the defining features of Indian culture are the realization of the underlying unity of life and the dominant spiritual motif, as argued by Coomaraswamy and Sri Aurobindo, then art should be an integral part of the national spirit.

In the Vedas, Coomaraswamy tells us, the practice of art is viewed as "a form of *yoga*" (1918: 24). Art is viewed in deeply psychological terms. For instance, *Agni Purāṇa* draws a connection between dream and art. The practice of visualization as referred to by Śaṅkarācārya is seen as identical in worship and in art (cf. ibid.: 27). The artist in order to be effective must realize four required moods of friendliness, compassion, sympathy and impartiality (cf. ibid.). He must meditate upon *śūnyatā* (non-existence) of all things. For, *yoga* is "not merely a mental exercise or religious discipline, but the most practical preparation for any undertaking whatever". For instance, Hanumān prays to the gods before he attempts to rescue Sītā in the Aśoka-Vāṭikā. In other words, art, ethics and spirituality go hand in hand in this scheme of things.

The aesthetic emotion (*rasa*) in the spectator *rasika* is carried through determinants (*vibhāva*), in Croce's words "physical stimulants", to aesthetic reproduction, consequents (*anubhāva*), "deliberate manifestation of feelings as gestures, etc.", mood (*bhāva*) thirty-three in number, "induced in the characters by pleasure and pain", "involuntary emotions" (*sattva bhāva*) 'emotional states originating in the inner nature. For the work of art to produce *rasa*, one of the permanent moods must form a master motif in which all other expressions of emotions are subordinated. Degree of excellence in poetry is discussed in *Kāvya Prakāśa* and *Sāhitya Darpaṇa*.

As Coomaraswamy asks rhetorically:

> What then is beauty, what is it that entitles us to speak of diverse works as beautiful or *rasavanta*? What is this sole quality which the most dissimilar works of art possess in common? Let us recall the history of a work of art. There is (1) an aesthetic emotion on the part of the original artist — the poet or creator; then (2) the internal expression of his intuition — the true creation or vision of beauty; (3) the indication of this by external signs (language) for the purpose of communication — the technical activity; and finally (4) the resulting stimulation of the critic (*rasika*) to reproduce of the original intuition or of some approximation to it.
>
> — 1918: 48

On the other hand, early Buddhist art is popular, sensuous and animistic. Gāndhāra art is a mixture of the Eastern and Western formulae. "Buddhist primitive" art exists in Amarnāth in India and Anurādhapura in Ceylon (Sri Lanka), thanks to "energy working in greater isolation".

For Coomaraswamy, the dance of Śiva is a manifestation of primal rhythmic energy that represents Śiva's main activities: *śṛṣṭi*, *sthithi* and *saṁhāra*. The dance is also symbolic of the world cycle.

Coomaraswamy is at his critical best when defending the many-armed images of Indian art. For instance, Vincent Smith finds Indian sculptures that adorn the medieval temples as "hideous" and "grotesque". Similarly, Maskell speaks of "these hideous deities with animal's heads and innumerable arms". Sir George Birdwood suggests that "the monstrous shape of the Purāṇic deities is unsuitable for the higher forms of artistic presentation" (Coomaraswamy 1918: 80).

Coomaraswamy refutes these charges as completely unfounded. A basic lack of understanding of the spiritual traditions of Indian art is behind such abysmal condemnation. And thus, European viewers are apt to be repelled by the sculpture of "Hiraṇyakaśipu". The truth, however, is that it depicts the splendid rendering of the well-known themes of the impious king who met his death at the hands of the avenging deity in man–lion form (ibid.: 83).

In turning to music, Coomaraswamy sees a similar difference in the attitude to music in the cross-cultural context. There is the European tradition of "Chamber music of an aristocratic society" *vis-à-vis* temple music where the musician is the spiritually inspired "Servant of God". We can understand this tradition with the help of *rāga* and *rāginī*. The *rāga* is a selection of five, six or seven notes distributed along the scale but the *rāga* is more particularized than a mode, for it has certain characteristic progression and a chief note to which the singer constantly returns (ibid.: 90). *Rāga*s are associated with rhythmic ritual of daily and seasonal life. The examples cited here are most telling. There is the parable of the singer who was forced to sing the Deepak Rāga, and tragically burst into flame, and the equally symbolic tale of Nārada who sang badly and the musical notes in the form of men and women lay "weeping over their broken arms and legs" (ibid.: 92). After all, the "Indian singer is a poet and the poet a singer".

Indian musicians are essentially mediums or channels for divine music.

This view of art also finds parallels in Tagore's conceptions spelt out in essays that are part of a collection called *Personality: Lectures Delivered in America* (1917). While arguing that art is created out of a surplus of emotions, Tagore went on to say:

> The greatness and Beauty of Oriental Art, especially in Japan and China, consist in this, that there the artists have seen this soul of things and they believe in it. The West may believe in the soul of Man, but it does not really believe that the Universe has a soul. Yet this is the belief of the East, and the whole mental contribution of the East to mankind is filled with the idea. So we in the East need not go into details and emphasize them; for the most important thing is this universal soul, for which Eastern sages have sat in meditation and for which Eastern artists have joined them through artistic realization. — quoted in Devy 2002: 46

VII

Sri Aurobindo has a relatively smaller but equally significant body of art criticism that has been mentioned earlier. Of the various art forms he does a closer analysis of forms of fine arts, sculpture and architecture while mentioning music in passing. Of literature, literary theory and criticism, he has written plentifully in his *Future Poetry*, earlier cultural writings and in his letters to poet disciples. Although not trained formally in the artistic tradition, Sri Aurobindo was exposed to the best of the Western and Indian art during his education in England as well as his Baroda days. He kept himself abreast of developments in art especially regarding the *Bengal School of Art*.

It is in the series of essays under what came to be known as *The National Value of Art* that Sri Aurobindo defines his concept of aesthetic nationalism. "The first and lowest use of art", says Sri Aurobindo "is purely aesthetic, the second is the intellectual or educative, the third and highest the spiritual" (2003: 439). Each plays an important role. The aesthetic aspect of life is of crucial importance. He observes:

> We do not ordinarily recognize how largely our sense of virtue is a sense of the beautiful in conduct and our sense of sin a sense of ugliness and deformity in conduct.
>
> — ibid.: 442

However, ethics and aesthetics have had a troubled relationship in the West. There were four gradations, Sri Aurobindo, says in the Greek ethical though:

> the *euprepis,* that which is seemly or outwardly decorous, the *dikaion,* that which is in accordance with *dike* or *nomos,* law, custom, standard of humanity based on the sense of fitness . . . , thirdly the *agathon,* the good based partly on the seemly and partly on the just and lawful, and reaching towards the purely beautiful; then finally the supreme *kalon,* that which is beautiful, the supreme standard. . . . The progress of ethics in Europe has been largely a struggle between the Greek sense of aesthetic beauty and the Christian sense of higher good. — ibid.: 443

Beyond the aesthetic and intellectual utility of art, there is the spiritual. For, "spirituality" he says, "is a wider thing than formal religion — and it is in the service of spirituality that Art reaches its highest self-expression" (ibid.: 450). Why is the cultivation of the arts important to the life of a nation. As Sri Aurobindo explains:

> It is not necessary that every man should be an artist. It is necessary that every man should have his artistic faculty developed, his taste trained, his sense of beauty and insight into form and colour and that which is expressed in form and colour, made habitually active, correct and sensitive.
>
> — ibid.: 153

Sri Aurobindo brings to bear on his essays and reviews such as "Two Pictures", "Indian Art and an Old Classic", "The Revival of Indian Art", "Rupam" and "South Indian Bronzes", his understanding of a spiritualized aesthetics and the role it can play creatively in the new Indian nation. And thus in *Shama'a* edited by Mrinalini Chattopadhyay, he singles out the English artist, J.D. Fergusson's "Rose Rhythm" and the accompanying article on his work by Charles Marriot. Sri Aurobindo finds in this portrait "a strong psychical truth". "The impression given is the materialization of a strong and vivid astral dream." The difference between this and the psychic manner in which the East will portray a similar imperssion will at once appear by turning to the "gracious and subtle Indian painting" in the first number (ibid.: 626).

The same aesthetic skill is displayed in Sri Aurobindo's review of O.C. Gangooly's *South Indian Bronzes*, "an opulent collection of nearly 100 fine plates preceded by five chapters of letterpress, one side of the artistic work of the south". Sri Aurobindo disproves the theory that divides the north and south on racial lines and posits instead the existence of two types of culture in ancient India. In discussing these bronzes, especially Naṭarāja, the Dancing Śiva in the "self-absorbed concentration, the motionless peace and joy", Sri Aurobindo alludes to the dominant spirit of Oriental art. "All characteristic Oriental art", he declares, "indeed seeks to go beyond the emotions and the senses: a Japanese landscape of snow and hill is as much as image of the soul as a Buddha or flame haired spirit of the thunderbolt" (ibid.: 582).

VIII

To conclude, Ananda Coomaraswamy and Sri Aurobindo manifest close parallels and some differences with regard to culture and nationalism. Products of the modern West, both critics turned to Indian sources in order to fashion a new national image. Decolonization was central to both. Yet both rejected forms of nativism or insular chauvinism. Instead, they espoused a cosmopolitanism firmly rooted in a critical understanding of Indian traditions. Coomaraswamy spent most of his career in the West with Western companions. Sri Aurobindo after early life in Baroda, and an active political life (1905-10) in Bengal, retired to Pondicherry to "the cave of *tapasyā*", where with the French mystic Mirra Alfassa, he worked out a new destiny for mankind, based on his theory of a future evolution of man. While Sri Aurobindo is more versatile in a multidisciplinary context, and takes up art criticism as part of his larger *oeuvre*, Coomaraswamy's knowledge of the history of arts is more focused and professional. Between the two, Coomaraswamy appears to be somewhat conservative in some areas of social living, yet both of them pioneered a radically new approach in the first half of the twentieth century.

Art historians need to make a fresh assessment of Coomaraswamy in the light of the criticism of Niharranjan Ray, K.G. Subramanyan, Amritanayagam and others. The analysis of the art scene in this context must cover the days of the *Company School of Art* during the height of the Raj, the role played by Rabindranath Tagore, his nephews and the brothers Gaganendranath and Abanindranath, and others like Nandalal Bose. Yet others such as art administrators like E.B. Havell, the Principal of Calcutta School of Art, institutions like the Visva Bharati at Santiniketan, played an equally important role in the resurgent interest in Indian art.

Although periodic assessment of the *Bengal Renaissance* continues to be made, art historians and critics need to make a similar evaluation of the contribution by early critics of Indian Art against the backdrop of *swaraj* in ideas. Sadly, both Sri Aurobindo and Coomaraswamy are neglected today, much to the detriment of theory and cultural criticism. It is hoped that a renewed interest in both *vis-à-vis* the role of the arts will help to create new directions in thought amongst the intellectuals of modern India.

References

Aurobindo, Sri, 1959, *The Foundations of Indian Culture*, Pondicherry: Sri Aurobindo Ashram.

———, 1993, *India's Rebirth*, Mysore: Mira, Aditi Centre.

———, 1997, *Essays Divine and Human* (*The Complete Works of Sri Aurobindo*, vol. 12), Pondicherry: Sri Aurobindo Ashram.

———, 2003, *Early Cultural Writings: The Complete Works of Sri Aurobindo*, vol. I, Pondicherry: Sri Aurobindo Ashram.

Coomaraswamy, Ananda, 1918, *The Dance of Shiva: Fourteen Indian Essays*, New York: Sunwise Turn Press.

Devy, G.N., 2002, *Indian Literary Criticism: Theory and Interpretation*, Hyderabad: Orient Longman.

Heehs, Peter, 1989, *Sri Aurobindo: A Brief Biography*, New Delhi: Oxford University Press.

Woodroffe, John, 1919, *Is India Civilized?: Essays on Indian Culture*, Madras, Ganesh and Co.

5

Towards an Understanding of the Aesthetical Philosophy of Coomaraswamy

Ranjan K. Ghosh

ANANDA Coomaraswamy is rightly regarded as a doyen among the modern thinkers on Indian art, philosophy and culture. His writings on these subjects bear the imprint of his own deep conviction and insights into these areas. His analysis of Indian art, at a time when the Western critics very often debunked it and spoke unfavourably about it as well, really paved the way for a proper appreciation and understanding of the genius of Indian creative fervour. This also helped restore the vast panorama of our artistic output to its lost glory. It is therefore relevant to take a closer look and also revisit his pioneering contribution to the fields of art and aesthetics. In what follows, an attempt will be made to bring out some of the salient points in his aesthetical philosophy.

It is important to bear in mind that Coomaraswamy characterizes Indian art as religion centric.

> Indian art is essentially religious. The conscious aim of Indian art is the intimation of Divinity. But the Infinite and Unconditioned cannot be expressed in finite terms; and art, unable to portray divinity unconditioned, and unwilling to be limited by the limitation of humanity, is in India dedicated to the representation of gods, who to finite man represent comprehensible aspects of an infinite whole.
>
> — Coomaraswamy 1981: 27-28

The content of such art is not mere imitation of nature or the phenomenal world. It is not merely a record of what the physical eye registers; rather, it seeks to capture the essential truth underlying the physical world of the senses. Implicit in this is an attempt to provide an insight into the objective and methodology of Indian art. In India creative engagement has been with the Infinite and the Unconditioned.

> India is wont to suggest the eternal and inexpressible infinites in terms of sensuous beauty. The love of man for woman or for nature is one with his love for God. . . . All life is a sacrament, no part of it more so than another, and there is no part of it that may not symbolize eternal and infinite things. In this great same-sightedness the opportunity for art is great. But in this religious art it must not be forgotten that life is not to be represented for its own sake, but for the sake of the Divine expressed in and through it. — 1981: 31

Art as much as religion is a way of looking at life. Art has a definite aim, function, and value both for artist and spectator. The Western idea of "art for art's sake" is neither applicable to nor acceptable by Indian art.

Now, to begin with the point that Indian works of art are not mere imitations of life or nature. What is reflected in these works is a quest for reality in terms of what may lie beyond the physical appearance. The artist of the old schools never drew from nature at all as he fell back on and made use of his store of memory pictures or images, his power of visualization, and his imagination. What is sought to be expressed is the idea behind sensuous appearance. The empirical reality is *māyā* (illusion). Nature to the Indian mind is a veil, *not* a complete revelation. Art is to be something more than a mere imitation of this *māyā*.

Realism when understood in terms of the imitation of an object actually seen at the time of the creative engagement is quite antipathetic to imagination, and it does not find a place in the ideal of Indian art. An important distinction is drawn between *ideal beauty* and *empirical beauty*. The latter is given as the retinal image and is given to the physical eye, while ideal beauty is given only as a *mental* image. As Coomaraswamy explains:

> But it is further possible, by imagination, the first and essential quality of genius, to apprehend ideas which, though subsisting in the cosmic consciousness, have not yet assumed and may never assume a physically visible form.

And, so:

> It is for the artist to portray the ideal world of true reality, the world of imagination, and not the phenomenal world perceived by the senses. — ibid.: 24

Artistic creativity is an intensely inward journey undertaken for the purpose of reaching out to the Ultimate Reality. While perhaps the physical reality holds sway on the mind of the Western artist, the Indian artist is given to the search of the Ultimate Reality which calls for treating art as a *spiritual* undertaking.

> Probably no truly Indian sculpture has been wrought direct from a living model, or any religious painting copied from the life. Possibly no Hindu artist of the old schools ever drew from nature at all. His store of memory pictures, his power of visualization and his imagination were for his purpose finer means; for he desired to suggest the idea behind sensuous appearance, not to give the detail of the seeming reality that was in truth but *māyā*, illusion. . . . Nature remains to the Hindu a veil, not a revelation; and art is to be something more than a mere imitation of this *māyā*, it is to manifest what lies behind. — ibid.: 21-22

Crucial to this enterprise is the attempt to discover and suggest the *Idea* behind the sensuous appearance. Plato, as we know, was critical of art, because art copies or imitates appearances. This criticism will apply to any art that seeks to imitate nature. But Indian art by not taking to this path escapes the criticism.

Coomaraswamy rightly points out that no truly Indian sculpture has been wrought direct from a living model, or any religious painting copied from life. For that matter, no Indian artist of the old schools perhaps ever drew directly from nature at all. Thus the mental or the *ideal* gets precedence over the empirical. The power of the *imagination* is capable of portraying the ideal world of true reality. It seeks to reach the type, or the Platonic Ideal. So the forms or images that are made are *archetypal*. In the Śilpaśāstras, there are elaborate rules or canons that are required to be followed in making the images. Rather than being particular, the images represent generalized or universalized types or forms. This also accounts for the absence of a tradition of portrait painting. Artistic creativity and reflective intuitiveness go hand in hand. Creative expression is both a means and an end in itself. Aesthetic communication is not a mere transmission of information or message; rather, it is the expression of the Divinity underlying the visible world.

The point we are trying to highlight is that a deep sense of idealism informs the methodology and objective of Indian art. In this regard the practice of art is a form of *yoga*. Indeed, in the Indian tradition of *rasa* theory, aesthetic emotion is regarded as akin to that which is felt when the phenomenal self perceives the transcendental Self. In Coomaraswamy's words:

> . . . the important part once played in Indian thought by the concept of art as *yoga*, [is] a subject sufficient in itself for a whole volume. It will be remembered that the purpose of *yoga* is mental concentration, carried so far as the overlooking of all distinction between the subject and the

> object of contemplation; a means of achieving harmony or unity of consciousness.

And also,

> . . . the later Hindu view which treats the practice of art as a form of *yoga*, and identifies aesthetic emotion with that felt when the self perceives the Self. — 1991: 26

Yoga as intense concentration of the mind is a means of achieving harmony or unity of consciousness — a state of consciousness in which the duality of the Self and the other ceases. It is by means of *yoga* that the artist finds it possible to "discover" the true nature of things. Coomaraswamy finds support for this view of art from Śilpaśāstras as he quotes Śukrācārya:

> Let the imager establish images in temples by *meditation* on the deities who are the objects of his devotion. . . . In no other way, not even by direct and immediate vision of an actual object, is it possible to be so absorbed in contemplation, as thus in the making of images. — ibid.: 24

Such inwardization of the visual image bears the stamp of "a spiritual discovery" rather than a creation (cf. Coomaraswamy 1981: 90). The artist "sees" the image in his mind's eye and seeks to represent his vision in terms of line and colour. Thus one can see the boldly executed images in Indian paintings with clearly drawn lines and contours without any vague or fuzzy details. The strong flowing lines are definitive in their character and the colours are applied flatly over the contoured areas. There is no deliberate attempt to create an illusion of three-dimensionality that characterizes the phenomenal reality.

The specimens of such art impart a value, an attitude to life, rather than imparting any instruction of a moral or other kind. Indian art is not didactic. Coomaraswamy is quite clear:

> Of course, a work of art may and often does afford us at the same time pleasure in a sensuous or moral way, but this sort of pleasure is derived directly from its material qualities, such as tone or texture, assonance, etc. or the ethical peculiarity of its theme, and not from its aesthetic qualities: the aesthetic experience is independent of this, and may even, as Dhanañjaya says, be derived in spite of sensuous or moral displeasure. — 1991: 34

There is thus a clear distinction drawn between aesthetic experience on one hand and sensuous pleasure and any moral or ethical message, on the other. The former is quite independent of the latter. In other words, the artist seeks to portray the ideal world of true reality, the world of imagination. The value imparted in and through such art is of a different order. In appreciating and understanding Indian art one has to learn to orient oneself to the inner vision of the ideal.

In Indian art, the ideal of beauty is a beauty of *type* — one that is formalized and rhythmic. Coomaraswamy raises the question with regard to the ideal of beauty in Indian art and then goes on to clarify the point.

> What is the ideal of beauty implicit in Indian art? It is a beauty of type, impersonal and aloof. It is not an ideal of varied individual beauty, but of one formalized and rhythmic. The canons insist again and again upon the ideal as the only true beauty. — 1981: 33-34

Further,

> The appeal of formalized ideal beauty is for the Indian mind always stronger than that of beauty associated with the accidental and unessential. The beauty of art, whether fictile or literary, is more compelling and deeper than that of nature herself. — ibid.: 34

As has been pointed out by P.N. Bose, Śilpaśāstras' *Śukranīti* maintains that an image should be such as would infuse the spirit of meditation in the heart of the onlooker (1978: 29). Such an image is *ideal* from the Indian point of view. Further, according to these Śilpaśāstras, an image to be beautiful must be in contemplative mood. This was regarded as the highest criterion of artistic beauty and excellence. Also, to make the images contemplative it is necessary that the artist should also be of a contemplative mood. The figures of the Buddhas of Sāranāth of the Gupta period are among the finest examples of such images in contemplative (*dhyāna*) mood.

Coomaraswamy points out that *dhyāna* and *yoga* play an important role in the practice of Indian art as well as for its thematic content. It has been said in the *Śukranīti* that the images of gods in this mood yield happiness to man. Because of such injunctions laid down in Indian Śilpaśāstras, Indian sculptors devoted all their attention to making images of gods. This is not to say that we do not find human figures. In the Bharhut or Sāñcī sculptures we do find human figures though they seem to occupy only a secondary position. Coomaraswamy acknowledges that this is why it has often been said by Western critics that Indian art is mostly canonical. Thus, (i) being canonical in nature, Indian art imposes upon itself severe restriction; and (ii) since the forms or images look similar, Indian art cannot lay claim to originality. But as has been pointed out by Coomaraswamy, even within the matrix of such canonical form there is enough scope of freedom for the artist to give sensuous expression to the non-sensuous and ideal form of reality. As to the charge that there is no originality in Indian art, it has been rightly said that there can be no absolutely original art just as there can be no absolutely new language for *communication* to become possible. Art that is altogether original can never be truly great. How can a single person supersede the "race imagining" of centuries?

> Art that is altogether original can never be truly great. How could one man's labour rival the results of centuries of race-imagining? The true material of art must ever be that which has already commanded the hearts of men rather than any fancy of the passing hour. — 1981: 48

We may now turn to another important Śilpaśāstra in which Yaśodharā lays down the following six limbs of the art of painting (*ṣaḍaṅga*) to which Coomaraswamy draws pointed reference:

> *rūpabheda pramāṇāni bhāvalakṣanam yojanam* ।
> *śādṛśya varṇikabheda iti citra ṣaḍaṅgakam* ॥
> — 1994: 181 fn. 14

The first one, *rūpa-bheda* (distinction of forms and appearances) is also suggestive of the methodology to be used by the artist. This requires a process of severe mental discipline of intense concentration by which the artist has to "see" and fix the form in his mind's eye. E.B. Havell draws a parallel to this by citing the famous parable in which Arjuna on being asked by his teacher Droṇa to describe the bird to be struck down replied that he saw only the bird's eye. Referring to this, Havell says:

> It is the same way in Indian art and in all Oriental art inspired by Indian idealism. The artist, through a process of severe mental discipline, is taught to discriminate the essentials in forms and appearances, and to see clearly with his mind's eye before he takes up brush or chisel.
> — 1920: 200

This is to underline the fact that the form to be executed as a painting or sculpture has to be clearly and unambiguously delineated in the mind's eye. It has been further suggested that *rūpa-bheda* is like the revelation of the divine or Śruti while the remaining five principles — proportion, expression, beauty, resemblance and use of material — are like Smṛti, the knowledge of which is handed down by tradition. Some more comments on the five principles would be in order here. *Pramāṇam*, which stands for measurement, proportions, etc. had been dealt with in various other Śilpaśāstras. *Śukranīti*, for instance, lays down that one should design for all the limbs a grace that is suited to them. In Māyāśāstra and *Pratimā-Lakṣaṇam*, a great deal of importance is given to the eyes and to the proportions of other limbs. According to *Śukranīti*, an image made as per the principles laid down by Śilpaśāstras is beautiful. There is also an acceptance of the fact that beauty and grace must come from the heart of the artist rather than by just following the canons in a routine manner. Thus Śilpaśāstras also give enough allowance for the freedom of the artist. These canons, however, were laid down keeping in mind the primary purpose and use of art, which was in order to make images that would help the worshippers in their worship. Indeed, *śilpa* in India was mainly dependent on *religion*.

The principles of *bhāva* and *lāvaṇya-yojanam* — i.e. feeling and beauty or grace — are linked to the heart or soul of the artist. Intense devotion on the part of the artist finds its expression in terms of *bhāva* and *lāvaṇya-yojanam*. The latter is often understood in the sense of saltiness. However, Niharranjan Ray works out another sense or interpretation and suggests that it stands for the quality of fresh butter and likens it to the *freshness* of youth.

Of the last two principles, *varṇikabhaṅga* has been generally understood in terms of the use of the medium or tools. The category of *sādṛśya* has to be understood not in the sense of imitation, but rather as what bears a reference to something in the world of senses; in the phenomenal world. In other words, the image must look familiar to the spectator on the basis of his common experience. Sri Aurobindo interprets *sādṛśya* as "the truth of the essence of the form" (1955: 242). It is by means of the inward vision of the Indian mind that such essence can be grasped or apprehended. Many of the specimens of Indian art make use of sex symbolism which however should be viewed in the overall context of the true spirit of Indian thought which draws no distinction between sacred and profane. Coomaraswamy elaborates the idea thus:

> By many students, the sex symbolism of some Indian religious art is misconceived; but to those who comprehend the true spirit of Indian thought, this symbolism drawn from the deepest emotional experiences is proof of the power and truth alike of religion and art. India draws no distinctions between sacred and profane love. All love is a divine mystery; it is the recognition of Unity. Indeed the whole distinction of sacred and profane is for India meaningless, and so it is that the relation of the soul to God may be conceived in terms of the passionate adoration of a woman for her lover. — 1981: 31-32

The relation of the soul to God is often conceived in terms of the passionate adoration of a woman for her lover. The actual embrace of the Divine figures represents the complete surrender of the soul to God. This may perhaps be said of many of the *mithuna* (erotic sculpture) figures at Khajurāho. Coomaraswamy points out:

> There are thus two main motifs in the sex-symbolism of Indian art, that may be represented by feminine conceptions, and even by the actual embrace of the Divine figures; these are the complete surrender of the soul to God — and the reaction between two aspects of a personal Divinity, whence is imagined to arise the whole phenomenal universe after submergence in the formless (*pralaya*). — ibid.: 32

There is thus this dominant view that the unity that runs through all Indian art has a spiritual end. Pointing to this, Coomaraswamy says that just as through all Indian schools of thought there runs like a golden thread the fundamental idealism of the Upaniṣads, the Vedānta, so in all Indian art there is a unity that underlies all its bewildering variety. The unifying principle here is also idealism. As Coomaraswamy says:

> The real aim, both of art and science, is to reach the type, the Platonic Idea. Art seeks this end deductively and synthetically, empirical science only inductively, and analytically. — ibid.: 19

Quite in line with this Sri Aurobindo has this to say:

> All Indian art is a throwing out of a certain profound self-vision formed by a going within to find out the surest significance of form and appearance, of discovery of the subject in one's deeper self, the giving of soul-form to that vision and a remoulding of the material and natural shape to express the psychic birth of it with the greatest possible purity and power of outline and the greatest possible concentrated rhythmic unity of significance in all the parts of an indivisible artistic whole. — 1955: 242

The world that is experienced by us through physical means is subject to mutation and decay, whereas the world beyond, which we are in search of, is of a more abiding nature. The latter is not given to our physical organs. Indian artists create idealized images rather than imitating the physical world. Art, here, steers clear of the extreme polarities of high realism on one hand and dry abstractionism, on the other. Tagore rightly draws a distinction between reality and realism. As he says:

> Art is the response of man's creative soul to the call of the real . . . and sums up that for the "naturally introspective mind of the Eastern artist the real appears in its ideal form of fulfillment. — 1961: 13-14

Such art symbolizes *idealized forms and emotions* that are at a remove from actually occurring emotions and visible forms. The viewer of such art must cast his mind into a contemplative mode in order to be able to respond to the deeper significance of the created vision.

And now let us recapitulate some of the important point. First, in India, as has been pointed out earlier, the earliest thinking on art begins with the idea that *chanda* (rhythm, harmony, balance, etc.) characterizes *śilpa* (art). Works of craft such as woodcarving and embroidery, were also considered as forms of art. At a later stage the intervention of the artist's mind (his thought and feeling) was regarded as essential for *lalita kalā* (fine arts) such as painting and sculpture. Artworks were used as decorative pieces on the wall; as to icons, and images for worship, or as symbols for communicating religious ideas, narratives and conceptions. However, apart from all these uses, the primary objective of art is to provide a special kind of joy (*ānandam*) that is considered quite akin to the experience of the Ultimate Reality (*brhamānubhūti*). But only a person with a sense of detachment or disinterestedness could gain access to such experience.

Second, it has been pointed out that Indian art does not seek to imitate nature or life as it is experienced by the physical senses. This is connected to the point with regard to the importance attached to the mental intervention by the artist in the making of the artwork. What is given to the physical senses (or the physical eye) and recorded as such remains bereft of the mental intervention by the experiencing subject. So, the higher arts or *lalita kalā*s are not only products of human skill and *chanda* but the artist through a process of idealization also imparts to it these two mental cognates that are contributed as unique features by the experiencing subject. The artist through a process of idealization does this. The artist not only sees through his physical eyes but also contemplates the object of perception in and through his mental eye; i.e. the images that are formed are not merely retinal but *mental* or *ideal*. When we look at an object intensely and our concentration is completely taken up with it we seek to go beyond the object or its physical representation. At this point our imagination takes over and creates an image out of it. The physical object or its image no longer remains important as there is a seeking after of what is as yet not manifest in or through the object. This leap beyond the physical reality is the thrust behind the creative impulse.

Third, it has been maintained, "the whole aim of art is the expression of *rasa*, i.e., passion . . ." (Coomaraswamy 1981: 27). Experiencing *rasa* involves calling to the mind a basic emotion without its *actual arousal*. From the Indian standpoint, it is this experience that is created in art and also what is experienced by the spectator. In response to the question as to the nature of aesthetic communication it may be made clear that such communication does not involve ordinary emotions, such as grief and sorrow. For the same reason the emotion of pathos that Vālmīki creates in the great epic, the *Rāmāyaṇa*, unlike actual grief, is enjoyable as *karuṇa rasa* by the reader or spectator. In other words, there are two different kinds of emotions: one that is so often confronted in real life, and the other that is experienced in art (or poetry). The latter is in the nature of *idealized* emotion — something that is a mental construct, and created (rather than actually suffered) by the poet. Emotions in real life affect us in various ways. Under their influence one is hardly free to contemplate and create anything. But when such emotion is idealized it is expressed in a creative product. One may draw upon one's own life experiences while creating art, but what finally comes through in the work is emotion that is transcendental in nature, and not that of the poet or artist. The artist does not express his own personal emotion; he creates emotion that is *generalized*.

Finally, emotion in art is of a different order and is acknowledged as *lokottara* (extra-mundane). Experiencing such emotion is always a matter of delight unlike emotions in real life that are pleasurable or painful depending upon the way such emotion is related by the individual to his or her life. The distinction is indeed crucial to our understanding of the nature of art and how it functions. In art, we are concerned with *idealized* emotions rather than actual or real emotions. The former constitute the object of *contemplation* for us, the latter are actually undergone and responded to in life through action and behaviour. In other words, while life provides the raw material for art, what are created are idealized emotions for the sake of our contemplation and understanding.

The concept of ideal emotion can also be understood by relating it to the concept of beauty. From the Indian thinkers' point of view, beauty can be understood only in terms of the effect it has on one's consciousness. An object of beauty is also a source of bliss (*ānanda*) that is of the nature of emotion. The experience of bliss that one derives from an object of beauty is short-lived and often not unmixed with pain or suffering. For example, beauty in nature is given alongside ugliness and mediocrity. One turns to art for bliss that is more lasting as well as pure or unmixed with pain or suffering. Art, in this sense, is identified as a vehicle for perfect and unmixed bliss. Beauty in nature is partial and not pure, beauty in art is perfect and pure. In this sense, beauty in art is ideal — that which is reconstituted by the imagination of the artist or poet. The point to note here is this: such a view clearly and strongly affirms the role of the mental intervention of the artist in the creative process. This also calls for disciplining the mind and the senses, so that one can qualify to become a creative artist. Thus for the artist such an understanding has an ethical value. Similarly, the viewers must also attune their minds and their senses to a comparable degree of discipline so as to be able to appreciate and enjoy such art.

To conclude, it bears recall that Coomaraswamy provides an interesting perspective for an understanding of Indian art. There is, no doubt, a value-graded structure that seems to lie underneath all such creative output. For example, even to be able to respond to a decorative piece one must bring to bear on it an attitude that precludes narrow selfish ends. Similarly, as one progresses towards greater refinement of one's imagination and mental attitudes there is access to the various dimensions of the treasure trove of Indian art. Coomaraswamy brings out the philosophical underpinnings of aesthetical thinking concerning Indian art and suggests what to look for and how to look at these priceless specimens of art.

References

Bose, P.N., 1978, *Principles of Indian Silpasastra* (with the Text of Mayaśāstra), Delhi: Bharatiya Publishing House.

Coomaraswamy, A.K., 1994, *The Transformation of Nature in Art*, Delhi: Munshiram Manoharlal.

———, 1991, *The Dance of Shiva*, New Delhi: Sagar Publications.

———, 1981, *Essays in National Idealism*, Delhi: Munshiram Manoharlal Publishers (1st Indian edn.).

Havell, E.B., 1920, *A Handbook of Indian Art*, London: John Murrey.

Sri Aurobindo, 1955, *The Foundations of Indian Culture*, Pondicherry.

Tagore, Rabindranath, 1961, "Art and Tradition", in P. Neogy (ed.), *Rabindranath Tagore on Art & Aesthetics (A Selection of Lectures, Essays, and Letters)*, New Delhi: Orient Longman.

6

Ananda Coomaraswamy on Art, Culture and Indianness

Archana Degaonkar

ANANDA Coomaraswamy has been a renowned art critic, an art historian and a critic of culture. He had the unique distinction of being intimately acquainted with Asian as well as European art forms. This acquaintance presupposed a deep understanding of the cultural as well as philosophical background of both kinds of arts. His writings bear out a close grasp of the Indian culture, patterns of thought and feeling, customs and beliefs, philosophy as well as folklore. A towering figure in the colonial period, Coomaraswamy was a pioneer in the domain of modern scholarship on Indian art. An authority in Indian painting and sculpture, he offered an aesthetic–cultural definition of Indian identity in the struggle for national independence. A collector of artworks as well as curator of a museum, he was naturally more particularly sensitive to visual art but his knowledge of Indian poetry was of equal depth. He was as well acquainted with the art traditions of India, as he was with the *prayoga* aspect of art in the visual field. However, it would be misleading to regard him as a mere commentator of Indian art and culture. His genius lies in providing an astonishingly vast spectrum of ideas related to the phenomenon of Indian art. In so doing, he may not have offered a "theory of art" in the technical sense, but he has raised for the very first time, a number of issues crucial to the understanding of Indian art and culture, which were never before brought to light.

It is customary to highlight the importance of Coomaraswamy's thought in the context of the Indian national movement. Indian philosophical writings during the colonial period present before us a discourse which is markedly self-conscious. This is due to the acute awareness of the sharp distinction between the self and the other that was beginning to emerge towards the end of the nineteenth century. Essential Indianness was the self, sought to be represented in this discourse with clearly delineated boundaries. The "other" was the British influence as reflected in thought, speech and action. The guiding principle of this writing was not simply to preserve the purity and authenticity of the Indian self by offering a lucid exposition of it. Also seen with this attempt is the added effort to highlight its merits, sometimes even to assert its superiority. In this sense, there has been a defence of the Indian perspective on art and aesthetics, Coomaraswamy being the figure in the forefront. Actually there are four Indian thinkers of the colonial period — K.C. Bhattacharya, M. Hiriyanna, Rabindranath Tagore and Ananda Coomaraswamy — who have offered a cogent defence of what might be termed as "Indian aesthetics".

Coomaraswamy, a Sinhalese Tamil brought up in England by an English mother, a scientist by profession, was an art lover and connoisseur of art at heart. During the first decade of the twentieth century, he realized during a visit to India the urgent need to protect and preserve the vast treasure of art therein. Very few places in the country remained unspoilt by the influence of Western civilization. The disease of consumerism had set in along with the introduction of the industrial culture. Cheap goods of ordinary quality flooded the markets and the genuine high-quality articles produced by locals lost out in the commercial competition. The spread of English education added deeply to the already existing problems, for now Indians started to lose the ability to appreciate their own culture with an independent mind. Coomaraswamy writes with feeling on this state of affairs in his early work thus:

> It is a marvel to me how any self-respecting people can endure for a day, not the system of government — but the system of education from which we suffer, a system which is a far deeper and more perpetual insult to our culture than any of the incidents in railway trains of which we hear so much. The Education-Court was little more than a gigantic advertisement of English schoolmasters and Messrs Macmillian. There was practically nothing Indian about it. It is not surprising that the products of such education do not care for Indian art. — 1911: 15

Coomaraswamy has argued for *swadeshi* not in politics as such but in our art and culture. He believed that nations were made not by merchants and leaders but by poets and artists. He therefore made this appeal:

> Try to believe in the regeneration of India through art, and not by politics and economics alone. — ibid.: 4

For him *swadeshi* was, more than anything else, a way of looking at life.

There is an unmistakable intensity about the feelings of nationalism which Coomaraswamy experienced and the indignation that he felt about the cultural degeneration brought about by the British rule. Even before visiting India in 1906, he had started the Ceylon Social Reform Society of which he was the president. He had initiated

> a movement for national education, the teaching of indigenous languages in all schools and the revival of indigenous arts, crafts and culture. He had also started a journal called *Ceylon National Review* given to the same objectives. — Ray 1984: 4

The significance of his work is clearly seen against the backdrop of British rule and its political and cultural implications. Nevertheless, clearly, that is not all. There is a substantial part of his writings on Indian art that has a timeless quality. It yields matchless insights regarding the nature of Indian art, craft and culture — insights that are relevant even today. There is much that we can learn and assimilate as individuals and as a society from the writings of Coomaraswamy, especially in the context of aesthetics and philosophy of art in the present-day world. It is the aim of this paper to identify the insights imparted by Coomaraswamy in order to gain a better understanding of the nature of art theory in general.

First, Coomaraswamy played a pivotal part in creating awareness within us of our own identity. He taught us to look at the world and at ourselves through our own eyes, in the place of imported vision. This is the giving of *dṛṣṭi*, which is our need even today in the cyber world of a constricted existence. He offered us indigenous parameters, indeed he made us aware that we have parameters of our own; that we are not simply passive objects for others to pass judgements on. Our art has an intrinsic worth and identity, without involving comparative references to Western art and culture. His understanding of the nature and function of Indian art is authentic as it is in keeping with our traditionally articulated conception and the associated ethos of art. *Agni Purāṇa*, known as the Encyclopaedia of Indian literature and culture, supports most of the claims of Coomaraswamy. This is what Agnideva in his *Agni Purāṇa* has to say about the nature and origin of poetry:

- The origin of poetic imagination is *loka-vyavahāra* and the knowledge of Vedaśāstra (p. 701).
- The fruit of an epic is the acquisition of the four *puruṣārthas* (p. 702).

- That divine indestructible, *sanātana*, beginningless and all-pervasive *para-Brahman* which is regarded as incomparable, conscious and flame-like, expresses its natural joy sometimes. The expression of this joy (*ānanda*) is described as consciousness, miracle (*rasa*) (p. 705).

The commentary on the above description of *rasa* adds that this meaning of *rasa* was not given by Bharatamuni in his *Nāṭyaśāstra*, but is found in the Upaniṣads when they proclaim *raso vai saḥ*. It is important to note that eminent writers of poetics, such as Abhinavagupta, Mammaṭa and Viśvanātha have followed the same path carved out by the *Agni Purāṇa* in the interpretation of the role and function of poetry.

Viśvanātha writes in his *Sāhityadarpaṇa* citing the testimony of the *Agni Purāṇa* about the superiority of poetry over even the Vedas.

> He points out the superiority of poetry over the Vedas as regards the attainment of the four *puruṣārthas*. The Vedas and the Śāstras are equally capable of leading to *dharma*; but poetry is superior to them in three points: 1. Vedas are dry and insipid; while poetry causes the highest pleasure; 2. The Vedas can be learnt with great difficulty; while poetry is comparatively very easy; 3. It is those of mature intellect only who can study the Vedas, while poetry can be learnt even by those whose intellect is tender (not developed).
>
> — **Kane 1951**: 4

1956 in reference.

It is important to notice that poetry helps in the attainment of *dharma*, according to Viśvanātha. Coomaraswamy follows the same trail of thought while explaining Indian art at large. The spiritual theme and the backdrop of the four *puruṣārthas* are always present in his commentary on Indian art. Art is a pathway to spiritual advancement, although it is playful and pleasurable. The aim of art in life is in tune with the calling of *dharma* and even the higher demands of *mokṣa*. The "refrain" of the song of art is always mystical–spiritual in nature. To this extent, Coomaraswamy is true to the *śāstrī* tradition present in India. This clearly shows in the classical allusions he cites while explaining even modern poetry. He writes in his article titled "Song-words of a Punjābī Singer" in the following way while interpreting a Punjābī song:

> How can I soften the heart of my lover, literally *kapaṭa kī gāṅṭh* (the knot in the heart) is again a lament of loneliness or separation: the phrase calls up the classic words of the *Muṇḍaka Upaniṣad*: "Of him who sees that which is the highest and the lowest — the knot of the heart (*hṛdaya-granthiḥ*) breaks — all his doubts are solved — and his works become nothing.

According to Coomaraswamy, the tone and temper of Indian art are primarily spiritual–mystical. He takes the support of Sanskrit poetics many times to justify his position. Similar is his approach while interpreting Indian sculpture. He laments the fact that no Western critic ever bothered to read Sanskrit texts enumerating the merits of good sculpture.

> So far as I am aware, some extraordinary oversight has prevented any European writer from seeking assistance in Sanskrit writings on the theory of aesthetics, or even in a study of the Śilpaśāstras. One would have supposed that these would have been made at least the foundation of a study of the theory and development of Indian art.
>
> — Coomaraswamy 1911: 59

However, contrary to what some of his critics have alleged, Coomaraswamy has not been a mere theoretician of art. Critics have accused him of taking a text-based doctrinal approach instead of concentrating on the aesthetic–practical side of art. For instance, Nihar Ranjan Ray has written thus:

> His (Coomaraswamy's) basic assumption, which he was inevitably and irresistibly led to, was that Indian aesthetics was based on doctrines, prescriptions and conventions of

> religions that were essentially intellectual and transcendental in character and idealistic in aim and purpose. This basic assumption led him inevitably to an undue and sometimes irrelevant emphasis on the literary, religious, symbolical and metaphysical content of Indian art at the expense of important imaginative and aesthetic considerations, namely, problems of artistic form and its evolution, and the changing human and social context of art. — 1984: 6

I think that Coomaraswamy has equally emphasized the *prayoga* aspect of our tradition along with the theoretical *śāstrī paramparā*. We cannot overlook the fact that he was an avid art lover who collected precious artworks. He was a distinguished art critic and the curator of a museum. All this bears out the fact that he had a direct contact with art, Indian as well as non-Indian. His concern for Indian art is far from merely theoretical. Actually, it is instructive to briefly compare his thought with that put forth by M. Hiriyanna in this respect.

M. Hiriyanna is a pioneering figure in the modern formulation of Indian aesthetics. His article "Art Experience" first appeared in 1919 offering a completely new perspective of Indian art theory. Even though the wealth of philosophical thought in India had generally been recognized, aesthetics was never perceived to be a concern of the Indian mind. In addition, Western taste was unable to grasp the significance and magnificence of Indian art. Against this background, Hiriyanna articulated his ideas regarding Indian theory of art. His scholarship in Indian philosophy and his ability to see intellectual connections between varied disciplines enabled him to offer a picture of Indian aesthetics in relation to the *dārśanika* line of thinking in the *śāstrī* tradition. The following observations can be made about his writings on this subject; he mentions almost as *pūrvapakṣa*, a remark made by Max Müller, "The idea of the beautiful in Nature did not exist in the Hindu mind" (Hiriyanna 1997: 1).

He also cites Max Müller's comment that India is a "nation of philosophers". Hiriyanna responds with his view that such vague and general statements are of little practical value if there is no relevant evidence to support them. If one collects evidence by studying deeply the areas of Indian logic, psychology and metaphysics, it will be useful not only for the Indian thought but for Universal philosophy: no doubt, the same is true in the spheres of ethics and aesthetics. As for the latter, Hiriyanna states his plan in clear words in his celebrated first article on Indian aesthetics:

> The object of the present paper is to indicate, however slightly it may be, the nature of the advance made by the Indians in one by — path of philosophy, viz., aesthetics or the inquiry into the character of beauty in Nature as well as in art.
>
> — Ibid.: 1-2

The tone of the paper is that of *khaṇḍana* of the *pūrvapakṣa* that clearly represented a bias harboured by the Western mind. In this light Hiriyanna attempts a construction of Indian thought regarding the aesthetic with the help of evidence. Hiriyanna writes:

> We have even more direct evidence in the numerous works in Sanskrit on poetics which, though their set purpose is only to elucidate the principles exemplified in poetry and the drama, yet furnish adequate data for constructing a theory of fine art in general. A consideration of the teachings of these works shows us that Indian aesthetics had its own history, and the process of its evolution, as may well be expected, followed closely that of general philosophy.
>
> — Ibid.: 2

In this passage, Hiriyanna has made two important claims. The first claim asserts that there was an Indian aesthetics with a history of its own and the second holds that the evolution of Indian aesthetics followed the development of Indian philosophy.

According to Hiriyanna, the most noticeable feature of Indian philosophy is the emphasis it places upon the influence that knowledge ought to have upon life. For Indians the aim of philosophical quest is not knowledge (*tattvajñāna*) but the attainment of *mokṣa*, which is true freedom. The Indian theory of art was constructed and viewed in the light of this true freedom.

There is an agreement over this point between the views of Hiriyanna and Ananda Coomaraswamy as Indian philosophers concerned with art. Ananda Coomaraswamy, following the same line of thought, pointed to the anonymity of the artist in the Oriental world as a quest for liberation from oneself. "All the force of this philosophy is directed against the delusion 'I am the doer'" (Coomaraswamy 1911: 41).

The two aspects of Indian philosophy which Hiriyanna finds important to explain before speaking of Indian art consist of the "*ātma* doctrine" of the Upaniṣads and the concept of the *jīvanmukta*. The *ātma* doctrine, in its essence means that whatever is, is one. This oneness is manifested "more clearly in the inner self of man than in the outer world" (Hiriyanna 1997: 3).

The point where Coomaraswamy differs from M. Hiriyanna concerns the actual demonstration of theory to works of art. M. Hiriyanna has been more concerned with the demonstration of the existence of Indian aesthetics. His concern has been primarily more theoretical and none the less significant for being so. He was after all responding to the claims of Westerners against the possibility of Indian aesthetics. In the writings of Coomaraswamy, on the other hand, we find numerous examples of the application of the canon of spirituality to actual artworks. This, in fact, is the salient feature of his thought; it is strengthened by his awesome knowledge of Indian art. His explanations make us "see" the worth and beauty of the work of under consideration.

Consider the following account he gives in the article "Facial Expression in Indian Sculpture":

> The ideal, which informs the most universally accepted Indian Gospel, is that of action without attachment. This view of life, thus expressed in words, is equally clearly stated in sculpture or painting representing human or divine beings engaged in strenuous action, but having at the same time upon the face an expression of unshaken peace. This peace may be equally expressed in a destroying Dharmapāla, in an embracing *Puruṣa* and *Prakṛti*, and in a meditating Buddha. — 1911: 71

A passage from *Christian and Oriental Philosophy of Art* explains this point further:

> If we are disturbed by what we call the "vacancy" of a Buddha's expression, ought we not to bear in mind that he is thought of as the Eye in the World, the impassable spectator of things as they really are, and that it would have been impertinent to have given him features moulded by human curiosity or passion? If it was, an artistic canon that veins and bones should not be made apparent, can we blame the Indian artist as an artist for not displaying such a knowledge of anatomy as might have evoked *our* admiration? If we know from authoritative sources that the lotus on which the Buddha sits or stands is not a botanical specimen, but the universal ground of existence inflorescent in the waters of its indefinite possibilities, how inappropriate it would have been to represent him in solid flesh precariously balanced on the surface of a real and fragile flower! — 1956: 47-48

In the case of paintings, Coomaraswamy is extremely vehement in his denouncement of Western influence. This has also to do with the typically Indian practices related to art. The very ways in which Indians traditionally regard painting and sculpture are radically different from those of the West. The way in which visual art was placed and viewed in everyday life in India differed substantially from the West:

> The modern method of painting pictures and sticking them indiscriminately on nails about the walls of houses comes as near perhaps to the absolute divorce of art from architecture as is possible; but it is not a sign of taste on which to congratulate the moderns. The old Indians knew better, that walls were to be painted on, and that the heart and centre of the temple was its image.
>
> — Coomaraswamy 1911: 48

Now of course we know that

> In India three arts only, poetry, music and architecture, have been recognized to be "absolute", independent or fine. Sculpture and painting are admitted to be dependent on, subordinate to or aspects of architecture. This statement is corroborated by the fact that it is in works on architecture that the arts of sculpture or painting are dealt with.
>
> — Pandey 1959: 603-04

It was Coomaraswamy who brought to our notice the typical Indian practice of art viewing and argued that it was relevant for understanding our art. It is no surprise, therefore, that Coomaraswamy points out the necessity of the knowledge of the culture in which the art was born, on the part of the spectator. Indian art must be seen with the eyes of an Indian; both the concepts of "how to see" and "what to see" must be guided by the native culture. Here I think Coomaraswamy anticipates the doctrine propounded by E.H. Gombrich in his famous work *"Art and Illusion"*.

One must be acquainted with Indian ways of life, Indian philosophy and the Indian notion of spirituality to be able to understand and appreciate Indian art. An art critic should saturate himself with Oriental traditions if he wishes to understand and enjoy Indian art. In this respect, European critics have failed miserably. They have failed to see any beauty in our art. There are cultural structures with the help of which the artist sees the world. There is no innocent eye. Acquaintance with the cultural background at least prepares us for the basic understanding of art from a certain culture.

Coomaraswamy advises the European critic by writing thus:

> Let us at least avoid the thought that it is given to us alone to know what are beauty and truth, we must realize that other men besides ourselves have sought their images, and sought them not as we now seek, outside ourselves, but in their own hearts. — 1911: 68

Cultural relativism is present in the entire sphere of art making as well as art appreciation. Unfortunately, we have borrowed our artistic "seeing" from the Western world and even today we have to make an effort to realize the significance of our art traditions.

We have trained ourselves to look at our cultural accomplishments with the help of an alien perspective. The effects of British educational influence persist. Therefore, we cannot do without the insights given by Coomaraswamy. He teaches us that traditional Indian art had more to do with knowledge than with feelings; and knowledge is the more enduring of the two:

> The modern aesthetician thinks that he has done enough if he "feels into" the work, since he holds that the secret of art resides in a peculiar sensibility outwardly manifested as an aesthetic urge to express and communicate a feeling; he does not realize that, ancient works of art were produced, devoutly indeed but primarily to serve a purpose and to communicate a gnosis. — 1956: 74

This is a timeless insight imparted by Coomaraswamy. It helps us grasp better many of our sculptures and paintings in a more solid and authentic manner. Consider some of the paintings of Rādhā and Kṛṣṇa. It is true that the colour schemes are exquisite. However, we cannot analyse these paintings in terms of mere "surfaces of colour". They are also vibrant with deep spirituality, which adds immeasurably to their aesthetic appeal.

It is also interesting to note Coomaraswamy's notion of culture. According to him, culture originates in work and not in play. Animals carry out activities guided purely by pleasure too. There is nothing distinctly human about such pleasure-oriented activities. At least culture is not to be defined in such terms. The distinctive mark of a man of culture lies in two things: he can distinguish superior artisanship; he also has an unhurried sense of detachment. Coomaraswamy writes:

> To define culture is perhaps a harder thing. Plato identified it with the capacity for immediate and instinctive discrimination between good and bad workmanship, of whatever sort; it is perhaps in this respect that the present age is least of all cultivated. We may expand this definition by including a certain quality of recollectedness or detachment, a capacity for stillness of mind and body (restlessness is essentially uncultured), and the power of penetrating mere externals in individual men or various races. Culture includes a view of life essentially balanced, where real and false values are not confused.
>
> — 1911: 25

These real values link with spiritual knowledge and the Indian artist has made every effort to capture this spiritual aspect in art, whether it is painting or sculpture. Oriental art, in general, does not aim at reproduction of nature. Rather, it has sought to express realities of life. It is creative and living art. It is important for us to remember this.

Most important is how Coomaraswamy defines culture as the backdrop of artisanship.

It is true that as a people we have lost first hand touch with artisanship. Coomaraswamy especially has in mind the era when artisans worked in the streets of small villages. Common people knew a lot about artisanship, about the quality of materials used because activities of artisans were part of the ordinary daily routine, not separated from the community as they are in an industrial society. Coomaraswamy approves of this handicraft aspect of culture because he believed it to promote the quality of reflectiveness. He sees a link of this style of life with the inward movement of the mind, towards greater peace and repose. He writes:

> One does not forget that the childhood of Christ was spent in a carpenter's shop, nor that two at least of India's greatest poets and religious teachers — Kabir and Tiruvalluvar — were weavers. — 1911: 29

The question may arise as to what this discussion has to do with issue of art. The simple answer is there is no art without artisanship. Artisans traditionally generate the basic material of the artist, such as paints, colours, musical instruments and so forth. Virgil Aldrich in his *The Philosophy of Art* has discussed extensively the close relationship between artisans and artists. Artisans, he writes, deal with the material, which is pregnant with tonal possibilities. These tones whether in music or in painting constitute the medium through which the artist expresses the content. For example, the same colour, say, yellow has a different visual quality in oil paint than in watercolour. The same musical note has different tonal qualities if played on different musical instruments like the *sitār* and the violin. These tonal qualities are the ingredients of the artistic medium. This explains the close relationship between the artisan and the artist. Makers of colours or the makers of musical instruments are as important to the domain of art as artists themselves. It is a well-known fact that a veteran singer like Kumar Gandharva personally supervised the making of his *tānapūrā*. The tonal qualities generated by the *tānapūrā*s were of great musical importance to him, as they were part of his style of singing. Just as there have been *gharānā*s of music similarly there have been traditions of artisans in our country. This whole system was disrupted by the British rule, which dealt a severe blow to our art practices. The industrial culture also contributed to the downfall of the handicrafts culture. Coomaraswamy is severely critical of the industrial culture, and himself has been the subject of criticism for over-emphasizing the merits of the pre-industrial style of life.

We can only say in his defence that he has eminent philosophical company in the form of Martin Heidegger who protested against the problems technology created. Heidegger too has discussed the philosophical superiority of the pre-industrial approach to life, and there is an unmistakable similarity between the main thrusts of their arguments. Heidegger points out that the original meaning of the Greek word *techne* from which the word technology derives was closely allied with the notion of bringing forth artistic skills and even knowledge. It connoted the sense of ease associated with expertise and knowing. He contrasts the traditional wind-mill with the modern generators of electricity, which expend water. The traditional windmill did not place any demands on the forces of nature. On the other hand, the generator places demands on the waters of a beautiful river like the Rhine. It turns the river, which has inspired soul-stirring poetry into a mere obedient water source that can be regarded as "standing reserve" for the commands of man. Technology reveals hidden power structures, which have altered irrevocably the relationship between man and nature. Even a river has changed from being dreamy and poetic to an entity which is at the disposal of human commercial demands. Heidegger expresses a disturbing thought that the same relation is likely to obtain between man and man, if we do not recognize the manipulative and controlling nature of modern industrial technology. He has hope in the form of art though; his understanding of art somehow remains distant from the issues of "thingliness".

Coomaraswamy, however, never loses sight of the material and practical side of art. For him it is the most important aspect of Indian art. Some mode of manufacture is associated with art making. There have been specific relations and vocations responsible for bringing forth the exquisite artworks of the classical and medieval period. The issue of profit making or commercial gain was not important there. Coomaraswamy brings this to our notice in the context of art:

> It is because the idea of manufacture for profit is bound up with the currently accepted industrial sociology that things in general are not well made and therefore also not beautiful. It is only when the maker of things is a maker of things by vocation, and not merely holding down a job, that the prices of things approximate to their real value. — 1956: 91

The patrons, the artisans and the artists whose vocation for life was art, together gave rise to the mesmerizing Indian art with all its purity and beauty. The work that they produced thus had little or no considerations of profit making. Coomaraswamy has this profound meaning to express when he wrote that culture originates in work. In an industrial society, work is not enjoyable because of the industrial set-up and the workman feels victimized by the system of profit. One can hardly expect pure art to develop in such a money-driven society. Heidegger was right in saying that after the Industrial Revolution relations between man and nature as well as those between man and man have changed. This has adversely affected the concept and quality of art. One cannot rightfully criticize Coomaraswamy for making Indian art period based in the face of the Heideggerian claim that even the River Rhine has not remained the same in the industrial culture. We have to understand that our sensibilities have changed with the times. Coomaraswamy makes us aware of the loss not just of art but of the loss of devout faith, the loss of a leisurely lifestyle and a secure, stable existence. He brings home awareness of our true human condition in the face of changing times.

The second component of culture — the quality of detachment — that Coomaraswamy mentions, is possible only in a highly-structured and deeply-devoted community. Only the members of such a community could experience that sense of calm and security as their function defined them. As Coomaraswamy writes:

> The whole position is bound up with a traditional view that also finds expression in the doctrine of the hereditary transmission of character and function, because of which man can die in peace, knowing that his work will be carried on by another representative. — 1956: 42

This is not a defence of the traditional social system, but recognition of the period-specific view of art and human life. It also brings to our notice the invaluable and non-repeatable, exclusive nature of Indian artworks that we possess. It is our national and cultural duty to respect and preserve them. It also imparts the valuable insight that the quality of human social life, its organization and emotional dynamics determine the strength of art it will create. A disintegrated, insipid and commercial society is likely to produce art, which is insane and superficial. Aesthetic issues are in this sense inseparable from the texture and stature of society.

Moreover, a "certain quality of detachment", which Coomaraswamy describes, is indeed hard to find in today's speedy, hassled world. If restlessness is uncultured, restlessness is the chief characteristic of the modern and post-modern society. A search for inwardness is definitely indicated here. We learn from him that the cultivation and development of artistic sensibility depends upon the kind of education that we impart to youngsters. There has to be *swaraj* in art and education. Certainly, we can make greater progress in this respect even in independent India.

In addition, a reaching to the spiritual roots of our ancient tradition seems inevitable. Coomaraswamy tried to understand the notion of Indianness in terms of our artistic and cultural practices, steeped as they were in the devout *rasa* of spirituality. It is important to remember that this was not all. He has taught us to appreciate the sheer beauty of our own art. His articles on Indian paintings bear this out substantially. He is sensitive not only to their thematic content but also to their formal and stylistic details. Essentially, he is a critic and a teacher in his approach, someone who has given us awareness of the beauty and the aesthetic excellence of our art traditions. He has literally taught us how to look at and appreciate traditional Indian paintings, as they sometimes depict serene beauty and calm which is typical of the Indian landscape. His articles titled "On Mughal and Rajput Paintings" and "Night Effects in Indian Pictures" and many others bear this out.

Coomaraswamy teaches us that "art is specifically human. None of those primitive peoples, past or present, whose culture we affect to despise and propose to amend, have dispensed with art" (1956: 92). We must have art in so far as we are human beings. This is a challenge in an increasingly techno-savvy society. Today there is no danger of the British rule, but the need to define ourselves as Indians presents itself anew in a world that is changing alarmingly fast. At this point Ananda Coomaraswamy offers an account of Indianness that is as valid and humane as it is attractive.

References

Agnideva, *Agnipurāṇa* (Hindi tr.), Gorakhpur: Geeta Press.

Coomaraswamy, Ananda K., 1911, *Art and Swadeshi*, Madras: The Guardian Press.

———, 1956, *Christian and Oriental Philosophy of Art*, New York: Dover Publications.

Hiriyanna, M., 1997, *Art Experience*, New Delhi: Indira Gandhi National Centre for the Arts.

Kane, P.V., 1956, *Sāhityadarpaṇa*, Bombay: Nirnaya Sagar Press (4th edn.) .

Pandey, K.C., 1959, *Comparative Aesthetics*, vol. 1: *Indian Aesthetics*, Varanasi: Chowkhamba Sanskrit Series.

Ray, Niharranjan, "The 'Life' of Coomarswamy: An Interpretation", *Parokṣa: Coomaraswamy Centenary Seminar Papers*, ed. Gulam Mohammed Sheikh et al., Delhi: Lalit Kala Akademi, 1984.

7

Coomaraswamy as a Metaphysician

R.C. Pradhan

ANANDA Coomaraswamy is not only a great philosopher of art and art historian, but also a great metaphysician who has explored the unity among many metaphysical and religious traditions. His understanding of Indian and Western metaphysical systems is phenomenal, as is the depth and sweep of his metaphysical thinking. Though he does not develop a metaphysical system on his own (cf. Coomaraswamy 1977: 433-35), he gives clear indications as to how metaphysics has to be thought out and in what way metaphysics can be the foundation of the human civilization. Coomaraswamy's interest in metaphysics is not just academic and analytical but creative, comparative and personal in view of the fact that he saw human unity writ large in the metaphysics of the Spirit.

Metaphysics of the Spirit

Coomaraswamy looks at metaphysics not just as an abstract system of categories and principles, but as the "language of the spirit". He writes:

> Holding with Heracleitus that the Word is common to all, and that Wisdom is to know the Will whereby all things are steered, I am convinced with Jeremias that the human cultures in all their diversity are but dialects of one and the

> same language of the Spirit, that there is a "common universe of discourse" transcending the differences of tongues.
>
> — Ibid: 434

Coomaraswamy thus holds that there is an underlying unity in all human thought and culture because of which it can be said that the different systems of thought and culture could be viewed as so many dialects of the same language of the spirit. This also shows his commitment to the metaphysics of the spirit which is manifested in different ways in the East as well as in the West.

Coomaraswamy's access to and mastery over the metaphysical traditions of the East and the West are impeccable and matchless. He has studied Indian metaphysical literature in depth just as he has completely mastered Greek and Christian religio-metaphysical literature. This is reflected in his erudite discourses collected under the title *Metaphysics* (Coomaraswamy 1977). The underlying theme of his metaphysical essays is the unity of the spirit which is the reality that underlies all phenomena. The same Infinite Reality which is the eternal principle (cf. ibid.: 3-21) is searched for by all religious metaphysics across the globe.

Coomaraswamy derives his metaphysical insights largely, though not exclusively, from the Vedāntic sources which have enriched his creative genius. Besides, he has been greatly influenced by such thinkers as the Buddha, Lao-tzu, Jesus Christ, St. Augustine, Plotinus and Eckhart. In his metaphysical quest for truth he has been inspired by almost all great religious and metaphysical traditions. According to him, the ultimate truth is not expressed in any particular language; it has been expressed in all languages known to mankind. The ultimate truth is not the exclusive possession of any particular system of thought or metaphysics. Therefore, according to Coomaraswamy, we must distinguish the "Supernal Sun of metaphysics" from the "physical sun" (ibid.: 6) of our ordinary experience, so that we can free the metaphysical truth from narrow linguistic and religious considerations. Thus Coomaraswamy holds a form of metaphysical universalism and monism that boldly proclaims the oneness of truth and reality.

Metaphysics, for Coomaraswamy, is not a set of abstract concepts divorced from experience. It is, in short, not a closed system that is dependent on dialectical reasoning, but a living doctrine much like *philosophia perennis*. He observes:

> Metaphysics is not a system, but a consistent doctrine; it is not merely concerned with conditioned and quantitative experience, but with universal possibility. . . . The ultimate reality of metaphysics is a supreme identity in which opposition of all contraries, even of being and non-being, is resolved; its "worlds" and "gods" are levels of reference and symbolic entities which are neither places nor individuals but states of being realizable within you.
>
> — ibid.: 6

Such being the nature of metaphysics, Coomaraswamy finds Vedānta to be the ideal metaphysical system, as it is rooted in our experience of the spiritual unity of the universe. The idea of the "supreme identity" is very much Advaitic in spirit because of which he finds Vedānta to be the "perennial philosophy" which speaks of the reality under the aspects of "eternity, universality and immutability" (ibid.).

The Vedāntic Legacy

Coomaraswamy returns to the Vedānta for his metaphysical explorations because of the latter's closeness to his temperament and training. It is to the Vedāntic roots that he finally comes back because Vedānta offers the wholesome doctrine of identity between the human self and the universal self. Besides, Vedānta as metaphysics fulfils a practical purpose. According to him, "Vedānta can be known only to the extent that it has been lived" (ibid.: 9). According to him, Vedānta as a universal metaphysics is not mere mysticism, nor is it a kind of psychology or *yoga*, but a full-fledged philosophy of life that teaches us how to live and attain the "gnosis of light".

The greatest metaphysical principle laid down by Vedānta, according to Coomaraswamy, is the dictum: "That art thou" (*tattvamasi*)" (ibid.: 10). This principle enunciates the great metaphysical truth of identity between the "Thou", the individual self and the "That", the supreme self which is, in Coomaraswamy's words "the *Brahman*, God in the general sense of Logos or Being, considered as the universal source of all Being" (ibid.: 10). Thus construed, the Upaniṣadic Doctrine of Identity lays the foundations of a metaphysics that brings the human individual, the *jīva*, closer to the supreme reality or being.

The Vedāntic metaphysics of self unfolds the reality of man, of the "I", within a cosmic framework such that it is linked to a universal self. The universal self or the *Brahman* holds the key to the understanding of man in a non-anthropocentric way, because it is only the cosmic principle of *Brahman* which brings out the meaning of the individual human self. Coomaraswamy explains this cosmocentric view of man in the form of imagery (cf. ibid.: 13) which is like this: "Let us imagine a field in which games are being played. It has at the centre the throne on which the royal spectator is seated, encircled by the players. Let us also imagine that all the players are linked to the spectator in an invisible way, being dependent on Him for their performances. In this imagery, the spectator is *Brahman* or God and the players are the human beings who are linked to the former because they are controlled by Him. Thus, our position in the world is like that of the players and we are inwardly controlled by God."

This imagery sounds more Dvaitic rather than Advaitic, but the central message is clear that the individual self has no independent existence and that there is only one central reality and that is *Brahman*. Man's actions in the world appear to be real and independent, but in reality they are dependent on the supreme self or cosmic spectator, the cosmic "eye" (cf. ibid.: 14) that oversees everything.

Coomaraswamy finds an echo of Vedānta in the Christian tradition where the relationship between man and God has been established, not by identity, but by a vital spiritual link. The Father and the Son are one in the cosmic sense as all human beings belong to the same divine order of things. Such a mystic vision is not unknown to Christianity. The Kingdom of the Heaven is placed within man in the same sense as the supreme self is seated within the individual self in the Vedāntic way of thinking. Using the spectator-imagery, Coomaraswamy writes:

> The spectator's pavilion is the Kingdom of Heaven that is within you, viz. in the "heart" (in all Oriental and ancient traditions it is not only the seat of the will but also of the pure intellect, the place where the marriage of heaven and earth is consummated); it is there only that the spectator can himself be seen by the contemplative. . . . — Ibid.: 18

Thus a fusion of Vedānta with Christianity can be found in the idea that man is the "son of God" (or "the son of immortality"). This is further echoed in Eckhart's saying:

> Eye wherewith I see God that is the same eye wherewith God sees in me; my eye and God's eye, that is one eye and one vision and one knowing and one love. — Ibid.: 19

For Coomaraswamy, Vedānta and Christianity both proclaim that the supreme reality is the centre of all existence and that we are all united with that reality by our own spiritual nature. That reality is the eternal reality above all time and change and is the anchor of our all moral and spiritual aspirations.

Time and Eternity

Coomaraswamy is very much interested in the metaphysics of time and eternity in view of his spectatorial view of the universe. For him, as for many metaphysicians in the Eastern and Western traditions, reality has both the temporal and the non-temporal dimensions, corresponding to the changing face of the phenomenal world and the non-changing nature of the supreme reality called *Brahman* or "God". He is impressed by the fact that in all philosophical traditions such as Hinduism, Buddhism, Christianity and Islam and also in the Greek as well as modern Western metaphysical traditions, the problem of time and eternity has occupied a central place. This is because in all these traditions there has been a constant struggle for supremacy between the temporal and the non-temporal reality. Coomaraswamy observes:

> "Time" is either all or any part of the continuum of the past and the future; or that present point of time (*nunc fluens*) that always distinguishes the two durations from one another. Eternity is either, from our temporal point of view a duration without beginning or end or, as it is in itself, that unextended point of time that is now (*nunc stans*). — 1990: 1

Thus time stands for one dimension of reality in which there is a succession of moments and is a continuum of durations. Eternity, however, transcends temporal succession and is the eternal now. It cannot be called everlasting, "but coincides with the real present or now of which temporal experience is impossible" (ibid.: 2). The succession of the temporal nows is, as Coomaraswamy puts it, a "matter of relativity; it is 'we' who move, while *the* now is unmoved, and only seems to move — much as the sun only seems to rise and set because the earth revolves" (ibid.: 2). Eternity is like the sun which does not move but appears to move because of our ignorance. Such is the nature of the eternal reality which is the pivot of all existence itself having no beginning or end. It is the Vedāntic

Brahman that has no location in time and yet is the anchor of all temporal phenomena.

Coomaraswamy's metaphysics of eternity (ibid.) is anchored in Vedānta because the latter has always proclaimed that our longing for worldly life is suffused with time and death from which we must seek liberation. The cycle of birth and death is symbolized by time in the Vedāntic thought. Eternity is the timeless *Brahman* that is beyond temporality and death. The timeless is not a mere absence of time, but the reality that can be conceived beyond all temporal categories. The Vedāntic notion of immortality is synonymous with timelessness because it is the latter that guarantees freedom from the sway of time. This search for liberation from temporality and evanescence also marks the Buddhist metaphysics of the eternal law or *dhamma*. Buddhism, no less than Vedānta, is concerned with the timelessness because of the sovereignty of the cycle of birth and death in the evanescent world (cf. ibid.: 22-33).

Coomaraswamy finds a reaffirmation of the Vedāntic notion of time in Christian and modern metaphysics of time wherein time is conceived of in terms of duration. Eternity is affirmed in Christian thought as the timeless Reality above all temporal changes. The Kingdom of the Heaven is above all temporal durations and so God is conceived as the eternal presence. But this presence is not a temporal presence. God is the creator of both time and the world. Hence he is outside time and history. As Meister Eckhart says:

> To speak of the world as being made by God yesterday or tomorrow were a folly in us; He makes the world and all things in this present now. . . . — quoted in ibid.: 80

Thus the notion of eternity is the same as the eternal now which is not a temporal concept at all. In God there is only one now which is the eternity itself.

In conformity with the metaphysics of the supreme reality, Coomaraswamy shapes his metaphysics of time and eternity in order to show that nothing in time is finally and transcendentally significant. It is the eternal reality that keeps our metaphysical hope alive because man in time seeks to get rid of the shackles of time. It is the timeless world of the divine reality which makes us hopeful of liberation from the world in time. Unless we can see reality *sub specie aeternitatis* as the eternal now we cannot escape the vagaries of time and so cannot fulfil our metaphysical hope of liberation (cf. ibid.).

Self and Liberation

Coomaraswamy insists on the possibility of liberation of the individual self, since he is convinced that liberation is possible if we mean by the latter that man is freed from time and its vagaries by transcending the cycle of birth and death. The Vedāntic notion of liberation has traditionally been conceived as a state of liberation from ignorance and bondage to the world in time. It is the state of identity of the self with the higher self and of realizing one's true nature as the *ātman*. Such a state is called *mokṣa* or *mukti* which is a state of being rather than a state of mind only. The state of liberation is well described by Coomaraswamy as the state of the self-realization or of realization of God within oneself. He writes:

> It is evident that the possibility of such a simultaneous regeneration rests upon the theoretical identity of the sacrificer's real being with that of the immanent deity, postulated in the dictum, "That art Thou". To sacrifice our self is to liberate the God within us. — 1977: 78

The liberation here referred to is the realization of God within us by denying the not-self as the reality, for "our end is to exchange our own limited manner of being 'So-and-so' for God's unlimited manner of being simply . . ." (ibid.: 80).

The concept of liberation has its echo not only in Buddhism where the *nirvāṇa* of the self is emphasized but also in Christianity where the self is supposed to be freed from the world by denying itself. The Christian Gospels talk of the death of the soul for saving the soul: "No man can be my disciple who hateth not . . . his soul" (Luke 14: 26); "he who hateth in this world shall keep it unto life eternal" (John 12: 25) and "whosoever seeks to save, shall lose" (Luke 9: 25) (quoted in ibid.: 84). Thus, for Coomaraswamy, the idea of liberation is present in all religious and spiritual traditions because of the fact that spirituality emphasizes the transcendence of the self into a higher existence.

The idea of transcendence is supposed to be the core of spiritual life, according to Coomaraswamy. Here transcendence means the self-naughting or self-denial as Coomaraswamy puts it. It is the denial of the lower self and affirmation of the "spiritual nature that is immeasurable, inconnumerable, infinite, and inaccessible to observation" (ibid.: 91). The higher self is identifiably the soul which is infinite and immeasurable. By realizing the spiritual nature of oneself, one rises above one's lower self. That is the very idea of transcendence. Because this idea is implicit in all religious and spiritual traditions, Coomarswamy calls it the universal doctrine of "self-naughting and self-sacrifice" (ibid.: 97).

The notion of self-negation or self-transcendence involves the notion of free will because only with the help of free will can one transcend one's own self, i.e. one can overcome one's own limitations, both physical and mental. The general notion of free will involves a sense of free choice regarding one's own actions. This is inevitable in view of the fact that we exercise freedom in choosing the course of action we intend to follow. This involves what may be called "self-denial" in a certain sense because we choose one action in lieu of another. Especially in moral actions we have to deny our desires and biological propensities in order to perform a morally worthy action. Morality thus involves self-denial. This is true of our spiritual life where a greater degree of denial is involved. Coomaraswamy defends free will in the following way:

> There is a free will, a will, that is unconstrained by anything external to its own nature; it is only "ours" to the extent that we have abandoned all that we mean in common sense by "ourselves" and our "own" willing. — ibid.: 91

Thus, there is freedom in denying ourselves and our motives and desires because of the fact that our self is unconstrained by the external world. Since we are selves which are free from external necessity, we are free beings in the transcendental sense.

There has always been a doubt whether human freedom can be guaranteed in a divinely determined world. This problem is very much true of Indian metaphysics as of Western metaphysics where there is an apparent conflict between divine necessity and individual freedom. Such a problem is easily dissolved by Coomaraswamy by showing that human freedom of choosing one's actions and overcoming one's own self is part of the free will which coexists with divine necessity. Divine necessity is compatible with human freedom for the very possibility of spiritual and moral life. If that were not so, then there would have been no place for a sinner becoming a saint or any hope of redemption from the world. Coomaraswamy says:

> The doctrine of self-naughting is therefore addressed to *all*, in measure of their capacity, and by no means only to those who have already formally abandoned name and lineage. It is not the saint, but the sinner, that is called upon to repent his existence. — ibid.: 106

The self-denial is a free act undertaken by the distressed self for its own spiritual redemption.

Silence and the Supreme Identity

Coomaraswamy highlights the doctrine of silence in metaphysics keeping in view his Vedāntic leanings. In the Vedāntic tradition there has been much emphasis on silence as the culminating point of all spiritual endeavour. Silence has been spoken of because of the fact that the *Brahman* is not a matter of linguistic utterance nor is it a matter of discursive thought. Language and mind have been taken to be limited (cf. *Kena Upaniṣad* I.3.6; *Taittirīya Upaniṣad* II.iv.1; *Muṇḍaka Upaniṣad* III.i.7) so far as our knowledge of *Brahman* is concerned, according to the Upaniṣads. That is why it has been said that the supreme identity which is *Brahman* remains beyond language and discursive thought.

That is to say, we cannot articulate the *Brahman* by any familiar terms even if we do manage to say what it is not. Language as a tool to describe the ultimate reality remains ever inadequate because of the fact that nothing ordinary can be ascribed to the *Brahman*. Both language and logic fail to make sense of *Brahman* except in the negative sense of denying the ordinary attributes to it.

The idea of silence may lead to some sort of mysticism because of the fact that there is inevitably something unsayable in our language (cf. Wittgenstein 1961: 6.522). This is corroborated not only in Indian metaphysics where there is eloquent reference to silence, as shown by Coomaraswamy, but also there is ample scope for the mystical in Western metaphysics where intellect and language are shown to be limited with regard to transcendent reality (cf. Coomaraswamy 1977: 209-19).

Coomaraswamy is one with the great masters of metaphysical thought on the idea that the life of man cannot be merely guided by reason or intellect and that there is a higher reality that needs to be known or experienced directly by one's total being. He accepts the sovereign rule of the spirit in all human affairs, keeping alive the hope of a spiritual journey towards a life of eternal verity. This eternal truth has been the cornerstone of Coomaraswamy's transcendental metaphysics.

To conclude, Coomaraswamy, the philosopher of art and beauty, meets the philosopher of truth and goodness in his all-inclusive metaphysical picture of the universe in which time meets eternity and the earth meets heaven. In his metaphysical picture, the Vedānta happily sits with Christianity and Buddhism without any conflict. This has been possible because of the synthesizing metaphysical genius of Coomaraswamy.

References

Coomaraswamy, A.K., 1977, *Coomaraswamy: 2 Collected Papers: Metaphysics*, ed. Roger Lipsey, New Jersey: Princeton University Press.

———, 1990, *Time and Eternity*, New Delhi: Indira Gandhi National Centre for Arts; Bangalore: Select Books.

Wittgenstein, Ludwig, 1961, *Tractatus Logico-Philosophicus*, tr. D.F. Pears and B.F. McGuinness, London: Routledge and Kegan Paul.

8

The Visual and the Material in Coomaraswamy's Art History

Sarada Natarajan

INDIAN art history as we know it today emerged as an independent discipline in the first decades of the twentieth century, forged in the fiery debates between anti-imperialist intellectuals and ideologues like E.B. Havell, Abanindranath Tagore, Rabindranath Tagore, Aurobindo Ghosh, Sister Nivedita and Ananda Coomaraswamy on the one hand, and the colonialist establishment on the other. Both "Indian art history" and its primary object — Indian art — are therefore "artefacts", in a manner of speaking, of the struggle for national self-determination. It is only when we delve into the politics of late nineteenth-century debates surrounding archaeology, industrial arts, crafts and fine arts in India that we understand the synthetic and entirely modern nature of this categorization. For example, late nineteenth-century colonial discourses and institutions routinely treated architectural and sculptural artefacts like the Sāñcī Stūpa, Coḷa bronzes and the Qutub Minar as *documents of history*. Even when these objects were apotheosized as monuments or museumized, their aesthetic value and the meanings they originally embodied faded into insignificance in the face of their status as historical documents and as appropriated symbols of colonial knowledge, power and benevolence. Rājpūt and Pahāḍī paintings circulated within the colonial bazaars as collectibles, souvenirs or crafts. James Fergusson, who pioneered a colonialist version of Indian art history through his systematic survey of Indian architecture, was constrained by imperialist ideology to view the architecture of the subcontinent through the "industrial" or "mechanical arts" perspective (cf. Fergusson 1899: 35).

It is in this context that "Indian art", a category constructed, legitimized and theorized by nationalist scholars, emerges in all its radical newness. Coomaraswamy, more than any other cultural revivalist, was responsible for constructing a persuasive *theoretical* framework within which "Indian art", a unified category with a massive geographical and historical sweep, could be viewed and interpreted. Though he began his engagement with the arts somewhat modestly as a Morrisian defender of native craftsmanship against the apathy and destructive economic practices of British imperialism, the scholar changed course to become the most significant theoretician to date of pre-modern Indian art.[1] So paradigmatic was his contribution and so long-lasting its effects that even today historians of pre-modern Indian art find themselves compelled to dismantle specific formulations in his work before they can provide alternative ones.[2]

The present critique, like the ones before it, originates from my long-term engagement and fascination with pre-modern Indian art. It forms part of a larger research project on the historiography of Indian art in which I analyse certain representational practices in a diverse range of narratives about visual artefacts. I am specifically interested in how different narratives, originating from different subject positions, deploying slightly or radically different epistemological frames, vary dramatically in their representations of what is

[1] For an analysis of Coomaraswamy's problematic recasting of Morrisian philosophy, see Lutchmansingh 1990: 35-48.

[2] See for example, specific critiques of Coomaraswamy formulations in Sheikh et al. 1984.

supposedly a universally accessible dimension of works of visual art; i.e. their material and visual qualities.

Coomaraswamy's writings on Indian art present a uniquely complicated case study in this context. So much of his mature work on art is devoted to a detailed exposition of iconography, symbolism and metaphysics that even a few sustained passages of art-historical description, plain and simple, are hard to come by. One is justified in arguing that something as mundane as art-historical description is not really the business of Coomaraswamy, the metaphysician—philosopher. However, what of Coomaraswamy, the connoisseur, collector, curator and catalogue writer? The basic qualifications for these professional positions that he occupied include an above-average sensitivity to the visual/material qualities of artworks, coupled with the linguistic skills to "present" these aspects to a lay audience through the written word.

Another paradox emerges when we consider Coomaraswamy's inimitable contribution towards the aestheticization of Indian art for modern Western audiences in the light of his ambivalent relationship with the very concept of aesthetics. In the sections that follow, I analyse these and other contradictions in Coomaraswamy's writings with a view to demonstrating the problematic nature of the scholar's approach to the visuality and materiality of his objects of study.

Coomaraswamy's Framework for Indian Art

Nationalist art historians launched a two-pronged attack against colonialist discourses and institutional practices with respect to Indian art. They criticized the near-sightedness and commercialism of British policies for engendering the decline of arts and crafts in the country. Simultaneously, they rejected the "archaeological" approach of official colonialist discourse in its interpretation of ancient Indian art. Havell and

Coomaraswamy offered their alternative idealist–aesthetic interpretation of Indian art as a way of looking at Indian art from "an Indian point of view". Before examining specific formulations in Coomaraswamy's writings on Indian art, I will summarize the salient characteristics of "Indian art" within the nationalist framework; this summary will serve to contextualize my subsequent analysis.

The nationalist conceptual scheme for "Indian art" was partly derivative, drawing heavily on nineteenth-century ideas and theories about fine arts in the West. The triadic structure of Indian art within the nationalist scheme, the association of art with intellect, the notion of "masterpieces" setting the standards for the canon, the embedding of art with discourses of nationhood and a sovereign cultural identity, the relocating of historical artefacts within the *aesthetic realm* — these aspects of the nationalist framework for Indian art echoed the Western counterpart. Simultaneously, the nationalists consciously distanced themselves from certain Western-modernist formulations about art. In the context of Indian art, Coomaraswamy rejected the notions of art as an autotelic activity, the artist as creative genius expressing his individuality, and the modern Western approach to aesthetics. Most importantly, the nationalists emphasized the dichotomy between the materialistic, secular modern West and spiritual, religious, "traditional" India. This perceived divide formed the very foundation of the idealist view of Indian art.

The most distinctive characteristic of nationalist art history was its idealistic orientation; Coomaraswamy and Havell posited a spiritual/ideal "essence" for all Indian art that transcended historical, geographical, ethnic, economic, socio-cultural, even religious differences. All the diverse material manifestations of Indian art, according to this construct, were embodiments of a single set of primordial ideas or ideals. Coomaraswamy identified *philosophia perrenis*, which he equated with Sanātana Dharma, as the source of the doctrines and ideals of Indian, Oriental and even Medieval Christian art. According to the scholar:

> . . . just as through all Indian schools of thought there runs like a golden thread the fundamental idealism of the Upaniṣads, the Vedānta, so in all Indian art there is a unity that underlies all its bewildering variety. This unifying principle is here also Idealism, and this must of necessity have been so, for the synthesis of Indian thought is one, not many. — Coomaraswamy 1981: 17

The Idealist Framework and the Flattening of Diversity

The idealist (or transcendentalist) framework for Indian art pioneered by Havell, Coomaraswamy and others established a paradigm that continues to influence certain deep structures embedded within art history. I want to foreground one set of related problems that, in my opinion, continues to have a residual impact on the way we do pre-modern art history today.

Because its primary agenda was to prove that Indian art, like the Indian nation itself, was a cohesive, autonomous, autochthonous entity, unified by a set of shared ideals, the idealist framework had a tendency to gloss over and underplay the very real *diversity* of artefactual production encountered across the subcontinent. When material artefacts produced in different media, originating in a wide variety of material and symbolic contexts, serving distinct, even changing functions throughout their histories, are coerced into embodying a single set of universal ideas, there is bound to be a lack of fit. Their existential and phenomenal particularity is sacrificed and they are diminished to the level of illustrations in the service of some transcendental *logos*.

The logocentric straightjacket of "unity" at the level of ideas and ideals had several important consequences for the study of Indian art, three of which I take up here. First of all, the very notion of a set of "transcendental" ideals that supposedly unified the diverse manifestations of Indian art had powerfully *normative* implications. Artworks and artistic practices that somehow contradicted this mandate, that were secular or tended towards naturalism, for example, were relegated to a lower position in the art historical canon. Coomaraswamy's disparagement of Mughal painting is a case in point. He relegates Mughal painting to the status of a "byway" (*deśī*) art form. The criteria that, according to him, make Mughal painting *deśī* is the "dated" and "localized" nature of the form; its time- and place-specific realism (cf. Coomaraswamy 1956b: 135). Coomaraswamy also clearly values the anonymity of the Rājpūt painter over the custom of Mughal artists to sign their names (cf. Coomaraswamy 1965: 127-28). Further, though Coomaraswamy claimed for these ideals a universal validity, cross-referencing them across continents, centuries and cultures, they were, in fact, a synthetic, modern interpretation of select strands of historically specific philosophies, both Eastern and Western.

Another consequence of the centrality given to ideals was the de-historicizing of artworks. The idealist framework, with its stress on timelessness, tended to treat the diversity of artistic production across the subcontinent, varying most obviously according to time period, region and cultural context, as epiphenomenal. The vital links between artworks and the specific historical, cultural and material circumstances of their production and reception were less important than the links between artworks and transhistorical ideas. According to Coomaraswamy:

> . . . the most significant element in any given work of art is precisely that aspect of it which may, and often does, persist unchanged throughout millennia and in widely separated areas; and the least significant, those accidental variations of style by which we are enabled to date a given work or

> even in some cases to attribute it to an individual artist.
>
> — Coomaraswamy 1989: 128

The quotation above suggests that the scholar's focus of interest was not individual artworks at all but generic or ideal *types* — like the Naṭarāja type and the Buddha type. Given this approach, it is not surprising that Coomaraswamy was impatient with the formal attributes that marked individual artworks as both unique and part of a larger sequence; for him:

> "style and stylistic sequences" were the accident of art, a product of "human idiosyncracy".
>
> — Coomaraswamy 1956b: 39

What is surprising, however, is that this lack of interest in historical specifics extended to the scholar's approach to the *content and meaning* of artworks as well. In a recent article on the shifting meanings of the Naṭarāja icon, Padma Kaimal challenges Coomaraswamy's authoritative interpretation of the familiar Coḷa bronze Naṭarāja image on multiple counts. Most relevant here is her charge that Coomaraswamy's hermeneutic "recovery" was based on the assumption that the icon had one original, static meaning that remained fixed throughout its thousand year-long history. Drawing on inscriptional and visual evidence, Kaimal argues convincingly that the image, always polysemic in nature, experienced a radical shift in meaning at a crucial point in its history. She demonstrates how the originally destructive connotations of early Naṭarāja images in the Tamil region were transformed, through the tenth–eleventh-century appropriation of Naṭarāja as a Coḷa emblem, into the *ānanda tāṇḍava* associations made famous in Coomaraswamy's writings (Kaimal 1999: 390-419).

Finally, the absolute primacy given to ideas and ideal forms in Coomaraswamy's interpretation of Indian art meant that the material, visual, tactile, technical and other non-representational aspects of individual works of art were relegated to a minor position. Even as it challenged the realist epistemology of colonial archaeology, the idealist framework perpetuated the divide between the form and meaning of its objects. Here, however, the values were reversed, with metaphysical essence subordinating phenomenal appearance. In the last section of this paper, I attempt to demonstrate that Coomaraswamy's uncompromising focus on the symbolism and metaphysics of artworks, on transcendental ideas related to ideal types rather than on specific manifestations, resulted in the diminished significance of visual and material attributes of art in his writing.

The Idealist Framework and Reception

Consider the structure of Coomaraswamy's article introducing a new acquisition of the Fogg Art Museum, a Rāgmālā painting representing Rāginī Bibhāsa/Vibhāsa (Coomaraswamy 1931: 14-16). This article was published in November 1931 and can therefore be considered a mature work by the scholar. It is titled quite simply, *A Rajput Painting*. I chose this rather obscure article over more philosophical elaborations like *Dance of Shiva* and art history surveys like *History of Indian and Indonesian Art* because of its limited and definite function — to "present", as briefly as possible, a *particular* work of art, a material acquisition by a modern museum, to a readership of Western art connoisseurs. The length of the article does not permit me to reproduce it in its entirety here. So I will summarize the paragraphs and quote relevant excerpts:

- In the first paragraph, Coomaraswamy introduces Indian musical modes and their relation to time of day, seasons and states of mind according to "Hindu rhetoricians". He introduces Rāgmālā poems and mentions that the painting under analysis is number 35 of such a series.

- The second brief paragraph establishes the close relationship between Indian music, poetry and the paintings — all expressing a common theme.
- The third paragraph has a summary description of the painting. An excerpt from this leads as follows:

> Bibhāsa Rāginī is a mode of which the burden is that of the full enjoyment of love in union. The picture represents the hero and heroine seated on a bed in the chamber of a palace: the former is shooting an arrow (using the lotus bow of the God of Love) at a cock that is crowing in the garden and has disturbed the lovers — a motif repeated in. . . . [Here Coomaraswamy mentions related works in other collections.] Two lines of Hindi text express the situation in a very beautiful way . . . [the author quotes the text in translation].

- In the next paragraph Coomaraswamy elaborates on the contents of the text: the identity of spiritual and physical love in Indian thought; the body compared to the *tapasvī*, with a detailed explanation of the metaphysical significance of metaphor "the worm becomes the ichneumon". As far as I can make out, neither the *tapasvī* nor the worm is represented in the painting.
- Paragraph six contains another fragment of description, quoted here:

> The present example, of about CE 1600, is essentially a painting, and not merely a coloured drawing; the solid forms and planes are architecturally established by the colour. This colour (red, yellow, green, white and black predominate) is stronger and more intense than in any other Indian painting: more suggestive of enamel or stained glass than of water colour. The drawing, though only the basis for the colour, is of the greatest interest:

> extraordinarily bold, its method is wholly one of allusion, rather than of representation. The statement is made up of parts that must be grasped as a whole, and in association, rather than by literal interpretation of their separate meaning.

The rest of this lengthy final paragraph is divided between establishing the antiquity and sophistication of this form of art and comparing its "language" with contemporaneous vernacular literary texts. "The longer one studies this literature and painting", Coomaraswamy concludes, "the deeper and fuller one finds its content."

What I want to establish through this somewhat cumbersome presentation of a typical Coomaraswamy text, is a certain lopsidedness in the scholar's narrative style. On the one hand, we are inundated with a wealth of detail about representational "content" — the symbolism and metaphysical significance of a work of art. On the other, Coomaraswamy's description of the formal and visual attributes of the painting is cursory, brusque and unappealing, almost as if the author derived no pleasure from viewing the work, or if he did, as if such pleasure should be banished from the narrative.

The Visible and the Visual

Why does so much of Coomaraswamy's writing seem to hover around, behind and above the works of art, rarely giving us the sense of the author's physical encounter with particular works? Why does the scholar devote 70 of the 80 pages of text in his Boston catalogue of Jaina paintings and manuscripts to elaborations of Jaina hagiography, cosmology and Jaina literary texts? (cf. Coomaraswamy 1924). Why does he hasten to conclude his passionately written article on the dance of Siva with this anticlimactic statement:

> So far I have refrained from all aesthetic criticism and have endeavoured only to translate the central thought of the

> conception of Śiva's dance from plastic to verbal expression, without reference to the beauty or imperfection of individual works?
> — Coomaraswamy 1981: 65

Coomaraswamy is in his element when he can "read" paintings and sculptures as if they were written texts. Even in his description of the Bibhāsa Rāginī, we sense an inexplicable urgency that drives the translation of the *visible* into the *legible*. Left decisively out of the account is an entire dimension of the work, non-representational, yet powerfully affective.

In his book *Confronting Images*, Georges Didi-Huberman makes a thought-provoking distinction between the *visible* and the *visual* in a work of art. Visible elements are decipherable aspects of the work, elements of representation and signification which provide a key to "translating" the artwork — rendering it *legible*, like a written text. *Visual* elements, on the other hand, are neither visible in the sense of "representing" something definite and meaningful, nor are they invisible, that is to say the abstract, literally "metaphysical", the out-of-the-frame dimension of the work. The *visual*, as this scholar formulates it, is the powerful "appearance" or "presence" of an artwork, an efficacious quality that exceeds the representational, the legible dimension. "Massive and deployed", the *visual* reaches out and implicates "the gaze of a subject, its history, its fantasies, its internal divisions". According to Didi-Huberman, encountering the *visual* dimension in a work requires:

> . . . a gaze that would not draw close only to discern and recognize, to name what it grasps at any cost — but would, first, distance itself a bit and abstain from clarifying everything immediately. Something like a suspended attention, a prolonged suspension of the moment of reaching conclusions. . . .

> There would also be, in this alternative, a dialectical moment — surely unthinkable in positivist terms — consisting of not-grasping the image, of letting oneself be grasped by it instead: *thus of letting go of one's knowledge about it.*
>
> — Didi-Huberman 2005: 16

If one can hazard an inference from his writings, such an approach would have been equally unthinkable for anti-positivist Coomaraswamy, for a number of reasons quite consistent with his approach to art and aesthetics.

In an article titled "Reactions to Art in India", the scholar constructs something like a "traditional" theory of spectatorship, likening the work of visual art to a *kāma-dhenu,* "yielding to the spectator just what he seeks from it or is capable of understanding" (Coomaraswamy 1956a: 108). Accordingly, he divides the types of spectator into the *paṇḍita,* who are "concerned about the correctness of iconography", the *bhakta,* who are "interested in the representation of holy themes as such", the *rasika* who are "moved by the expression of *bhāva* and *rasa*", expressing "appreciation in the technical terminology of rhetoric", the *ācārya,* the fellow artists "who regard chiefly the drawing, and technical skill in general", and finally the *alpa-buddhi-jana,* "the ordinary laymen" who "like the bright colors, or marvel at the artists dexterity" (ibid.: 108-09). Coomaraswamy himself increasingly aligns with the *paṇḍita* in his later works; simultaneously, he distances himself from the apparently "superficial" delights of the *alpa-buddhi-jana.*

The scholar's reluctance to acknowledge the power of the visual and material was also directly connected with his distrust of "aesthetics" in its Western *avatāra* — as something that primarily stimulates or "irritates" the senses. In his view, traditional works of art, "were not produced for the delectation of the senses" but were geared to higher rational and spiritual ends (Coomaraswamy 1956b: 16). (Incidentally,

Didi-Huberman characterizes the *visual* as the irrational underside of artworks.) Coomaraswamy repeatedly dismissed what he called the aesthetic/sentimental approach to art, arguing that through its "intelligibility and functional efficacy", true/traditional art appeals ultimately to reason and not to the senses (cf. ibid.: 178).

It is ironic, then, that it was Coomaraswamy, more than any other person or institution, who was responsible for the aestheticization of Indian art in the West in the first half of the twentieth century. Was his emphasis on content over form, on the metaphysics and symbolism of Indian art, his way of neutralizing the reifying context of the modern museum and its tendency to render the sacred profane? This hypothesis is weakened when we take into account a somewhat neglected sphere of Coomaraswamy's art critical practice; his photographs.

In an intriguing article titled "The Other Half of Indian Art History: A Study of Photographic Illustrations in Orientalist and Nationalist Texts", Lee Lawrence excavates an interesting paradox in Coomaraswamy's approach to photographic visuals in his books (cf. Lawrence 2004: 287-314). Unlike most art historians before him, Coomaraswamy personally took or at least supervised many of the photographs used in his own books. Using a few examples, Lawrence argues convincingly that Coomaraswamy systematically adopts a modern, Western aesthetic for framing and lighting his photographs. In this last section, I expand on Lee's argument using a few illustrations found in Coomaraswamy's early photographic opus titled *Viśvakarmā* (see Coomaraswamy 1914).

Coomaraswamy's photographs (black and white) of Indian sculptures published in his 1914 book *Viśvakarmā* clearly demonstrate the operation of a Western (even modernist Western) aesthetic sensibility. The unorthodox profile view (*fig.* 8.1) of Prajñāpāramitā, for example, goes against the way

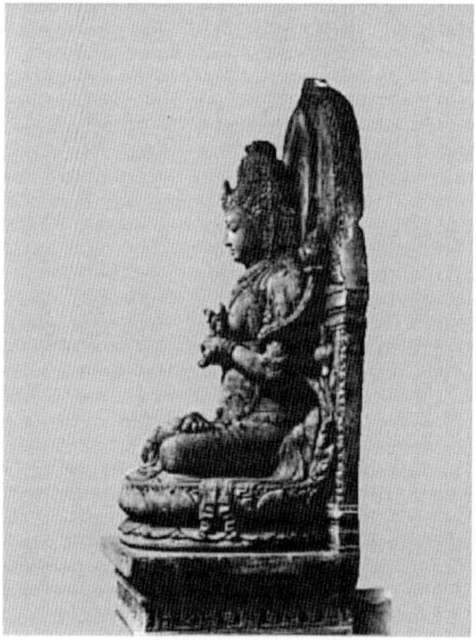

fig. 8.1: Prajñāpāramitā

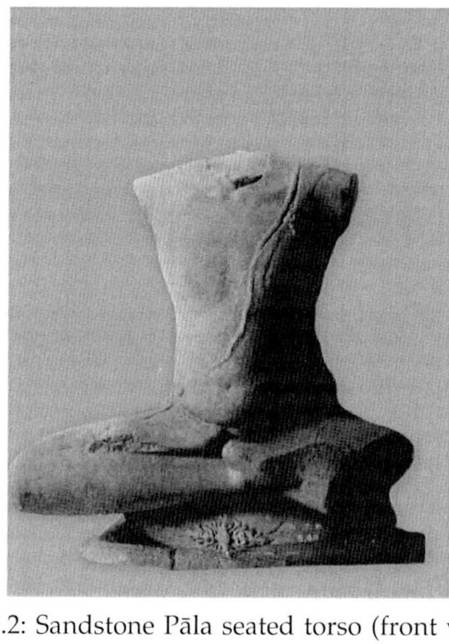

fig. 8.2: Sandstone Pāla seated torso (front view)

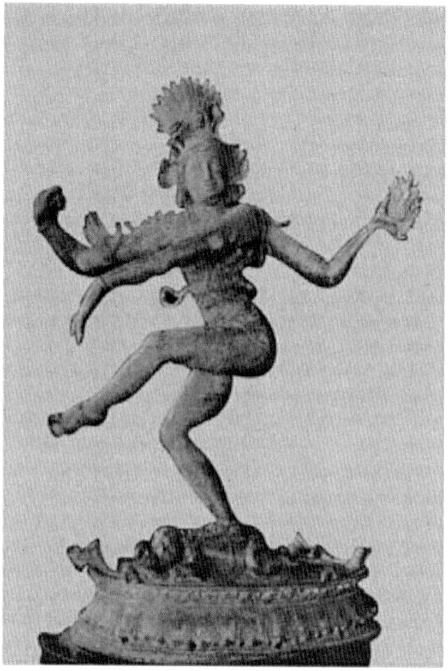

fig. 8.3: Madras Museum Naṭarāja

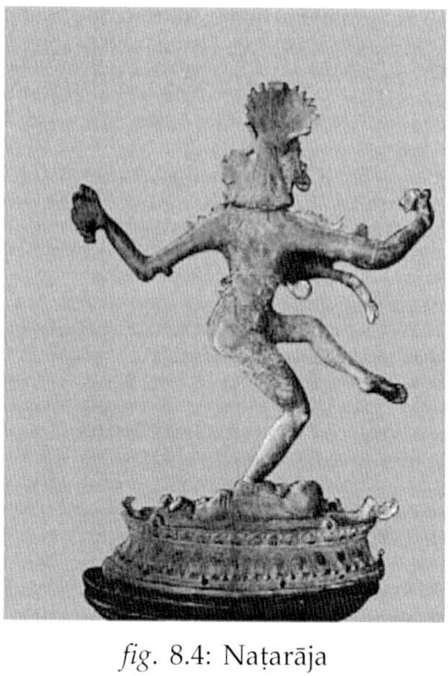

fig. 8.4: Naṭarāja

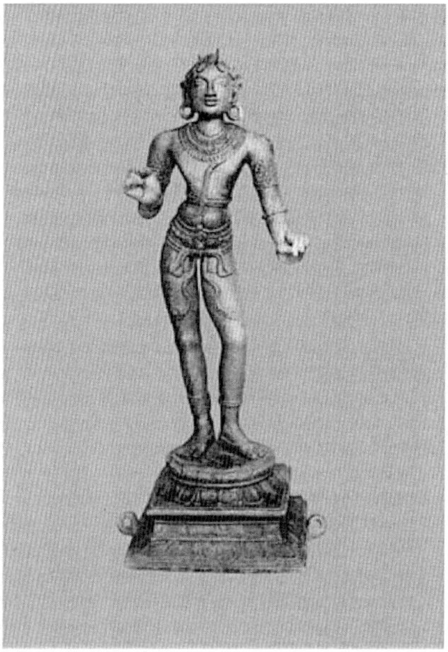

fig. 8.5: Sundaramūrti Nayanār Svami

in which the sculpture was "intended" to be viewed. The badly damaged sandstone seated torso from the Calcutta Museum (*fig.* 8.2), lit dramatically (in keeping with the Western convention for modelling 3-D form from the Renaissance onwards) from its front and its right, would have, in a traditional context been discarded as "unfit for use". Another startling "recto–verso" photograph of a patinated Naṭarāja (*figs.* 8.3 and 8.4) from the Madras Museum contradicts how the image would be viewed in its ritual context — burnished to a golden colour, clothed in silk and bejewelled, with the back view de-emphasized. Similarly, Coomaraswamy's minimal and starkly beautiful Sundaramūrti Nayanār (*fig.* 8.5) is invariably draped in a silk *veṣṭi,* one figure amongst 62 other bronze icons, in the icon's "original" religious setting in a Tamil Śaiva temple.

References

Coomaraswamy, Ananda, 1914, *Viśvakarmā*, first series, London: Messrs Luzac.

———, 1918, *The Dance of Siva*, New York: The Sunwise Turn.

———, 1924, *Catalogue of the Indian Collections in the Museum of Fine Arts*, Boston: Museum of Fine Arts.

———, 1931, "A Rajput Painting", *Bulletin of the Art Museum*, **1**(1).

———, 1956a, *The Transformation of Nature in Art*, New York: Dover Publications.

———, 1956b, *Christian and Oriental Philosophy of Art*, New York: Dover Publications.

———, 1965, *History of Indian and Indonesian Art*, New York: Dover Publications.

———, 1981, *Essays in National Idealism*, New Delhi: Munshiram Manoharlal.

———, 1989, *What Is Civilization?* Delhi: Oxford University Press.

Didi-Huberman, Georges, 2005, *Confronting Images*, tr. John Goodman, Pennsylvania: Pennsylvania State University Press.

Fergusson, James, 1899, *History of Indian and Eastern Architecture*, vol. 1, New York: Dodd, Mead and Company.

Kaimal, Padma, 1999, "Shiva Nataraja: Shifting Meanings of an Icon", *The Art Bulletin*, **81**(3): 390-419.

Lawrence, Lee, 2004, "The Other Half of Indian Art History: A Study of Photographic Illustrations in Orientalist and Nationalist Texts", *Visual Resources*, **XX**(4): 287-314.

Lutchmansingh, Larry D., 1990, "Ananda Coomaraswamy and William Morris", *The Journal of the William Morris Society*, **IX**(1): 35-48.

Sheikh, Gulammohammed et al. (eds.), 1984, *Parokṣa: Coomaraswamy Centenary Seminar Papers*, New Delhi: Lalit Kala Akademi.

Index